ONE FLESH
ONE HEART

ONE FLESH ONE HEART

Putting Celestial Love
into Your Temple Marriage

DR. CARLFRED BRODERICK

Deseret Book

Salt Lake City, Utah

No part of this book may be reproduced in any
form or by any means without permission in writing
from the publisher, Deseret Book Company,
P.O. Box 30178, Salt Lake City, Utah 84130.
Deseret Book is a registered trademark of
Deseret Book Company, Inc.

First printing February 1986
Second printing June 1986

Library of Congress Cataloging-in-Publication Data

Broderick, Carlfred Bartholomew.
    One flesh, one heart.

    Includes index.
    1. Marriage—Religious aspects—Mormon Church.
2. Mormon Church—Doctrines.   3. Church of Jesus Christ
of Latter-day Saints—Doctrines.   I. Title.
BX8641.B76   1986   248.4'8933204   85-29329
ISBN 0-87579-010-0

*To my
eternal companion,
Kathleen*

CONTENTS

PREFACE

Some years ago I decided that I ought to write a book based on the principles of successful marital relationships I had learned in my career as a marriage counselor. It was written for a general audience and published by a secular press. My assumption was that few Latter-day Saints would buy it because it was not aimed at them and did not use the language and rhetoric of the gospel. To my surprise, while it did reasonably well in the general market, it became a best-seller among the Saints.

On one occasion a distinguished Latter-day Saint colleague was asked to comment on the book and said, "Oh, I suppose it is a good book and does some good but it has nothing of Christ or his gospel in it." My defense at that time was that it was my observation (borne out by the sales of the book among the Saints) that Mormons had telestial problems in their marriages just like any other group and that it was appropriate to apply telestial principles to telestial problems. By the time they had progressed to a terrestrial level of marital relationship, I argued, they didn't need a book to help them the rest of the way to the celestial kingdom.

At the time I remember feeling somewhat smugly that my rebuttal had been clever and very nearly irrefutable. Since then I have repented of that opinion. I still believe that the basic principles of psychology, telestial though they may be, can help couples overcome their everyday telestial problems. But, with more experience, especially as a stake president working with troubled couples in my charge, I have come to believe that there are also higher principles that "advanced" couples need to master on their way to becoming a celestial unit. Thus this book.

One Flesh, One Heart: Putting Celestial Love into Your Temple Marriage is not for everyone. It presumes an audience that is committed to the gospel of Jesus Christ and to an eternal marriage. It assumes that even such couples may yet find room for improvement and sometimes even experience frustrating disappointment in that unique relationship, which is supposed to be their greatest source of support and satisfaction. It comprises just about everything I have learned about how to be married "in the Lord's own way."

I am deeply indebted to my secretary, Barbara McConville, who typed every word of every draft of the manuscript of this book and gave me encouragement as she typed.

INTRODUCTION

The quest for an eternal union can be understood only in the context of our quest for eternal life. Four choices between life and death determine the destiny of every son and daughter of God. The first was presented to us in the council in heaven: Would we elect to follow the Father and vow obedience and fidelity to him or would we follow the Usurper? Part of that first pivotal decision involved accepting the plan of the Father with its provision for our temporary exile to an unjust world, deprived of our memory of heaven and subject to every temptation and tragedy. It involved, I believe, our making a reciprocal covenant with our Elder Brother. He agreed to make it possible for us to find our way back from this exile as exalted beings, though at the cost of his own infinite sacrifice on our behalf. In return we covenanted to accept him as our Savior and our God, and to sacrifice whatever should be required of us by him in our mortal sojourn. I suppose we understood even then that when the time came, he would indeed be required to sacrifice everything for us while each of us would be called upon to sacrifice only according to our abilities. Of some, such as Job and Abraham and Joseph Smith and Spencer W. Kimball, much would be required. Of others, less; but whatever might be required, whatever pain or loss or humiliation, we acknowledged in advance that the requirement would be just and more than just. Our indebtedness is infinite, and any claim upon us is always less—far less.

It is recorded that two thirds of the Father's children made that initial choice for Life. We were among them. Our reward was, literally, to breathe the breath of life on this telestial globe. The other third chose death and will remain forever unembodied spirits.

The second critical choice-point came in this life. Would we follow the promptings of the Spirit of Christ until it led us to the authorized servants of our Father, and would we accept at their hand baptism, that ordinance of new life of which God has said, "Inasmuch as ye were born into the world by water, and blood, and the spirit, which I have made, and so became of dust a living soul, even so ye must be born again into the kingdom of heaven, of water, and of the Spirit, and be cleansed by blood, even the blood of mine Only Begotten; that ye might be sanctified from all sin, and enjoy the words of eternal life in this world, and eternal life in the world to come, even immortal glory.... Therefore it is given to abide in you; the record of heaven; the Comforter;... that which quickeneth all things, which maketh alive all things." (Moses 6:59, 61.)

We are taught that every man and woman will have this opportunity to choose between spiritual life or death, either in this second estate on earth or in its spirit-world extension: "The Spirit giveth light to every man that cometh into the world; and the Spirit enlighteneth every man through the world, that hearkeneth to the voice of the Spirit. And everyone that hearkeneth to the voice of the Spirit cometh unto God, even the Father. And the Father teacheth him of the covenant which he has renewed and confirmed upon you, which is confirmed upon you for your sakes, and not for your sakes only, but for the sake of the whole world.... And whoso receiveth not my voice is not acquainted with my voice, and is not of me. And by this you may know the righteous from the wicked." (D&C 84:46-48, 52-53.)

Those whose mortal circumstances have not permitted them the opportunity to accept or reject the kingdom are explicitly provided for: "All who have died without a knowledge of this gospel, who would have received it if they had been permitted to tarry, shall be heirs of the celestial kingdom of God; also all that shall die henceforth without a knowledge of it, who would have received it with all their hearts, shall be

heirs of the kingdom; for I, the Lord, will judge all men according to their works, according to the desire of their hearts."
(D&C 137:7-9.) Or, as the Psalmist put it, "Your heart shall live
that seek God." (Psalm 69:32.) And as Paul added, "For to be
carnally minded is death." (Romans 8:6.)

The third life-and-death crossroads on the path to eternal
life is the new and everlasting covenant of marriage, "for no
one can reject this covenant and be permitted to enter into
my glory," said the Lord. (D&C 132:4.)

The fourth is the choice to endure in that covenant in
righteousness unto the end. The promises made to those who
take upon themselves the responsibilities of an eternal marriage and magnify those responsibilities and endure to the end
are the greatest of all promises made by God to his children:
"They shall pass by the angels, and the gods, which are set
there, to their exaltation and glory in all things, as hath been
sealed upon their heads, which glory shall be a fulness and a
continuation of the seeds forever and ever. Then shall they be
gods, because they have no end; therefore shall they be from
everlasting to everlasting, because they continue; then shall
they be above all, because all things are subject unto them.
Then shall they be gods, because they have all power, and the
angels are subject unto them." (D&C 132:19-20.) Then the Lord
goes on to say: "Except ye abide my law ye cannot attain unto
this glory. For strait is the gate, and narrow the way that leadeth
unto the exaltation and continuation of the *lives,* and few there
be that find it. . . . This is eternal *lives*—to know the only wise
and true God, and Jesus Christ, whom he hath sent. I am he.
Receive ye, therefore, my law. Broad is the gate, and wide the
way that leadeth to the *deaths*; and many there are that go in
thereat, because they receive me not, neither do they abide
my law." (D&C 132:21-22, 24-25; emphasis added.)

All who read this book have made the first of these life-and-
death choices and have chosen life. Most who read it have also
made the second and the third choices. Indeed, they can point
to the records of their having made those choices before God
and at least two authorized witnesses. In the waters of baptism
they offered up their heart to God that they might live, and at

an altar in God's house they joined with another to covenant to become an eternal patriarchal unit. The fourth decision, to endure to the end, has no such moment of consummation. It is a decision renewed each week at the table of the Lord's Supper and each day with morning and evening prayer. The final evaluation of our having chosen eternal life over its alternative is reserved for our final report when we meet with our Father at the veil. The entire canon of scripture and the whole organization of the Church is dedicated to providing us inspiration and direction on our path toward that final meeting.

In view of that I offer my own observations on some of the principles and pitfalls along that path with much humility. Yet I have been privileged to share the joy and pain of many good people and to profit from their experience as well as my own. I feel an obligation to pass on the things that I have learned. My prayer is that they may be useful to Latter-day Saint couples who are truly seeking to become one flesh and one heart.

CHAPTER 1

"THEY SHALL BE ONE FLESH"

The marital relationship is different from every other relationship in creation. Of it and only of it did God decree that the partners should become one flesh. In plain language, at the core of the husband-wife relationship is a sexual and procreative joining.

The scriptural account of the creation places no other human stewardship before this one: "I, God, created man in mine own image, in the image of mine Only Begotten created I him; male and female created I them. And I, God, blessed them, and said unto them: Be fruitful, and multiply. . . And I, God, saw everything that I had made, and, behold, all things which I had made were very good." (Moses 2:27-28, 31.) When Adam was presented with his wife, Eve, he exclaimed: "This I know now is bone of my bones, and flesh of my flesh. . . . Therefore shall a man leave his father and mother, and shall cleave unto his wife; and they shall be one flesh. And they were both naked, the man and his wife, and were not ashamed." (Moses 3:23-25.)

Subsequently the drama in the garden of Eden was played out. Satan tempted Eve to become wise through partaking of the Tree of the Knowledge of Good and Evil: "When the woman saw that the tree was good for food, and that it became pleasant to the eyes, and a tree to be desired to make her wise, she took of the fruit thereof, and did eat, and also gave unto her husband with her, and he did eat. And the eyes of them both were opened, and they knew that they had been naked. And

they sewed fig-leaves together and made themselves aprons."
(Moses 4:12-13.)

I have always been intrigued with the symbolic features of
that part of the story. To me, the aprons of fig leaves Adam
and Eve fashioned after the fall in response to their new aware-
ness of their nakedness have always seemed fitting symbols of
the double nature of our sexual and generative stewardship.

On the one hand, in covering nakedness, the aprons suggest
the principles of modesty, chastity, self-control, and fidelity.
On the other hand, the fact that these aprons were made of
green, living leaves suggests the couple's assumption of the
godly power of fertility; of the lively, expressive, dynamic as-
pects of our sexual and procreative stewardship. As Lehi noted,
"If Adam had not transgressed he would not have fallen, but
he would have remained in the garden of Eden. . . . And they
would have had no children; wherefore they would have remained in a state of innocence, having no joy, for they knew
no misery; doing no good, for they knew no sin. . . . Adam fell
that men might be; and men are, that they might have joy."
(2 Nephi 2:22-23, 25; see also Moses 5:11; 6:48.)

But it is one thing to receive the injunction to be one flesh
and another to know how to achieve that goal. On one occasion
a bishop and his wife came to see me because their marriage
was falling apart. Among their mutual complaints was that sex
had been a disaster from the beginning of their marriage. What
made it worse was the husband felt that good Latter-day Saints
shouldn't have such problems. He believed that if anyone
should have a model marriage, the bishop and his wife should.
In fact, virtually everyone in the ward assumed that they were
the perfect couple, and he felt both hypocritical and a little
bitter that the image was false.

"President," he said to me, "show me the justice of it. We
keep all of the commandments. We pay a full tithe and a lot
more. We keep the Word of Wisdom. We were chaste before
our marriage and have been faithful since. Neither of us has
ever refused a call. We attend the temple regularly. We try to
be missionaries to our neighbors. And despite all of this, we

are miserably unhappy with each other and have a lousy sex life. That's not the way it's supposed to work out, President."

I took out my Doctrine and Covenants, turned to section 130, and read verses 20 and 21 aloud: "There is a law, irrevocably decreed in heaven before the foundations of this world, upon which all blessings are predicated—and when we obtain any blessing from God, it is by obedience to that law upon which it is predicated." Then I asked, "You say you have kept the law of tithing?"

"Fully."

"And you have received the blessings promised by that law?"

He looked at his wife and answered, "Yes, we have been richly blessed in that department."

"You keep the Word of Wisdom?"

"Scrupulously—well, maybe some overeating."

"And have you received the blessings associated with keeping that law?"

"Yes, we have been healthy as a family."

"So, it seems that you have been blessed for the laws you have kept. But the law of tithing and the Word of Wisdom are not the laws governing sexual fulfillment or marital happiness. When you have kept *those* laws you will reap *those* blessings."

As I reviewed with them the scriptural guidelines pertaining to their situation, they confessed that they observed almost none of the principles that underlie the blessing of a joyful sexual oneness.

Throughout the ages the prophets have exhibited a reticence to discuss this intimate aspect of the marital bond. I do not believe that this should be interpreted as prudery but rather as a measure of the respect they all share for that most sacred sacramental union. It is clearly intended to be the *private* and *personal* stewardship of the couple themselves. To make it a topic of public discussion or display (as has become common in our day) is to violate its sacred nature.

Indeed, almost the only circumstances in which these matters are discussed at all openly in the scriptures are in the context of counseling the Saints that a strong sexual bond between a man and his wife is a powerful resource in resisting extramarital temptation. In that context, however, Paul and others have provided us with strong guidance on the righteous conduct of this part of our lives.

For example, in his first letter to the Corinthians, Paul answered a question (the exact content of which we can only guess) as follows: "Concerning the things whereof ye wrote unto me, saying, It is good for a man not to touch a woman. Nevertheless, I say, to avoid fornication, let every man have his own wife, and let every woman have her own husband. Let the husband render unto the wife due benevolence [in the context of this passage Paul is clearly referring to the husband's attending to his wife's affectional and sexual needs]: and likewise also the wife unto the husband." (1 Corinthians 7:1-3, JST.)

So the point Paul makes is that our intimate life together ought to be kind, "benevolent." There is no room for coercion or neglect, for pressure or vengeful withholding. I suppose it must be granted that sex that is motivated *solely* by kindness would be missing a number of essential vitamins, but it is also true that sex lacking this quality does not meet the minimum standard of acceptability for Latter-day Saint marriages. So that ought to be our first step in shaping our intimate life together to the model of righteousness set forth by the spokesmen of the Lord: Nothing should be done except in kindness.

Paul goes on to say, "The wife hath not power of her own body, but the husband: and likewise also the husband hath not power of his own body, but the wife." (1 Corinthians 7:4.) That concept sets a very high standard indeed for lovemaking. To feel that when we are in the hands of our mate we are as safe as when we are in our own care, to be able to be perfectly trusting because we have found each other perfectly trust-worthy—what could be a more celestial standard?

I am probably one of the ten most ticklish persons in America. No one in my family would dare tickle Daddy because his responses are so explosive. Early in their lives my children discovered that their fun-loving, generally unflappable father

4

was transformed instantly into a killer gorilla when tickled. Yet I cannot tickle myself. The reason is that I trust myself completely. I know exactly what my fingers are going to do to my ribs, and when and how much. There are never any nasty surprises. In order for us to follow Paul's counsel to relate to each other such that "the wife hath not power of her own body, but the husband: and likewise also the husband hath not power of his own body, but the wife," each partner would have to trust the other as they trust themselves.

The third component of a righteous sex life, according to Paul, is *duty*. In the King James Version he counsels, "Defraud ye not one the other." That is, do not cheat each other by withholding sexually. In the Inspired Version, Joseph Smith used the alternative phrase "depart ye not one from the other." In either phrasing the meaning is clear from the remainder of the verse: "except it be with consent for a time, that ye may give yourselves to fasting and prayer; and come together again, that Satan tempt you not for your incontinency." (1 Corinthians 7:5.)

In the Church I have worked with many couples where a disenchanted wife or a passive-aggressive husband has withheld sex as part of a power struggle with their spouse. Many are the excuses, but the most common is, "I just don't *feel* like making love when we have all of these other unresolved problems." If I understand Paul's point, this part of marriage should *never* be permitted to become a weapon between a man and his wife. Part of the covenant of marriage is to become one flesh. We promise to do so. Since we take the view that absolutely no extramarital sex of any kind is to be tolerated, it is reasonable that the marital contract provide legitimate, regular opportunities for righteous sexual expression. To withhold that resource is, Paul says, to let "Satan tempt you . . . for your incontinency." To put it differently, it is a sin to send a husband or wife out into this seductive world unprotected from the temptations there by a satisfying, loving, sexual bond at home. Having attended many Church courts, I am persuaded that often the guilt for the sin of infidelity must be shared by the withholding spouse of the offender.

Kindness, trust (and its reciprocal, trustworthiness), and duty, then, are three of the qualities of a righteous sex life. Yet the perceptive reader will recognize immediately that as crucial as those virtues are, there is yet another quality that marriages must include if they are to be wholly satisfying. Where is the romance, the excitement, the ecstasy? Happily, the scriptures are not silent on that point either. No one expresses the thought more beautifully than Solomon as he warns his son against adultery and through poetic imagery (and some plain language) urges him to keep the romance in his marriage alive and vibrant:

> My son, attend unto my wisdom, and bow thine ear to my understanding: that thou mayest regard discretion, and that thy lips may keep knowledge. For the lips of a strange woman drop as an honeycomb, and her mouth is smoother than oil: but her end is bitter as wormwood, sharp as a twoedged sword. Her feet go down to death; her steps take hold on hell. . . . Drink waters out of thine own cistern, and running waters out of thine own well. Let [not] thy fountains be dispersed abroad, and rivers of waters in the streets. . . . Let thy fountain be blessed: and rejoice with the wife of thy youth. Let her be as the living hind and pleasant roe [the hind or roe is a type of antelope admired for its grace and beauty]; let her breasts satisfy thee at all times; and be thou ravished always with her love. (Proverbs 5:1-5, 15-16, 18-19.)

So the fourth component of a righteous sexual bond is the romantic component. Some couples in the Church have been concerned about sexual activities that might be considered unnatural or unholy.

In this matter, as in other spiritual matters, such as keeping the Sabbath Day holy or paying a full tithe, the *principle* is laid out clearly and each couple is left to work out the details with the Lord.

For example, at tithing settlement, the bishop does not provide you with a form to fill out, listing all of your income and all of your deductions to determine the authorized net gain upon which you must pay tithes. He asks, simply and straightforwardly, "Are you a full-tithe payer?" The answer is yes or no, and the burden is fully on the shoulders of the member to work out the arithmetic righteously.

Similarly, if the bishop should ask in an interview whether a couple keeps the Sabbath Day holy, he is not likely to read a checklist of approved and disapproved activities. Rather, he lets the couple decide, within the guidelines given in scripture and the counsel of the Brethren, whether the answer is yes or no.

In the same way, a couple should follow the promptings of the Spirit about sexual matters. This does not free them to make up their own rules any more than they are free to do so in the matter of tithing or Sabbath keeping. Rather, it frees them to seek out the will of the Lord on the matter, to take spiritual responsibility for their own decisions.

The general principles to be followed are beautifully set out by Paul in the opening verses of the twelfth chapter of his epistle to the Romans: "I beseech you therefore, brethren, by the mercies of God, that ye present your bodies a living sacrifice, holy, acceptable unto God, which is your reasonable service. And be not conformed to this world: but be ye transformed by the renewing of your mind, that ye may prove what is that good, and acceptable, and perfect, will of God." (Romans 12:1-2.)

If a couple will take that scripture for their guide, I testify that they will find the unity, grace, and joy in their intimate relationship that can occur only when their union is blessed by God and attended by the Spirit.

Couples who feel that this particular stewardship is not prospering may wish to counsel together, reviewing each of the four major issues outlined by Paul and Solomon and prayerfully considering what their goals in each area might be.

Similarly, couples who are uneasy as to whether their sexual activities fully meet the standard of being natural and holy might prayerfully consider changing that part of their lives. If that involves some sacrifice, as it does for some couples, they might recall that God feels it "reasonable" to require that we "present [our] bodies a living sacrifice, holy, acceptable unto God." Indeed, we have explicitly convenanted to sacrifice whatever is required of us. My own observation is that, despite our fears to the contrary, the Lord always makes it impossible to put him in our debt. Whatever we give up, he increases our blessings so that the sacrifice is, in the end, no sacrifice at all.

It is an unhappy fact that many fine couples in the Church face special problems in this area. Perhaps only a bishop or a stake president can fully appreciate the reality that behind the smiling, competent faces of many in the congregation are private troubles and sometimes tragedies that affect their sexual lives.

First, a distressing number of women (and some men also) have experienced incest or rape or some other upsetting and demeaning sexual experience. Depending on their age at the time of the occurrence, the nature of the experience, whether it was a single incident or a continuing nightmare, and depending also on the personality and temperament of the victim, the damage done to the person's self-confidence and sexual attitudes may be great or small.

Where the damage is great, it will require great patience and understanding from the spouse. Often a wise, understanding, spiritual friend of the same sex can be a helpful confidante and give the wounded person a chance to talk out her (or his) fears and resentments and inhibitions. Seasoned, compassionate priesthood leaders can be helpful (although, through inexperience it is also possible to be less than helpful). If professional counselors who share a gospel perspective are available, they too may provide a valuable service. The most important thing to know is this: there is no wound so deep that faith and patient, well-directed effort cannot heal.

A second issue that comes up more often than the ordinary, faithful Church member might believe is that one of the partners suffers from compulsive sexual thoughts or behaviors that are distressing to those who have them and upsetting to their partners. These thoughts and behaviors seem to defeat every effort of the couple or of concerned priesthood leaders to bring them under control. Among the most common are compulsive masturbation, reading of pornography, cross-sex dressing, and homosexuality, although these in no way exhaust the sad list.

In order to understand this illness it is important to distinguish mere weakness in the face of temptation from a true compulsion, which may prompt a person to considerable heights of ingenuity to persist in the problem. These sexual obsessions are similar, in the way they persist against all efforts, to substance abuse (such as compulsive drinking, smoking, overeating, or pill-popping) or to certain other unfortunate symptoms such as compulsive stealing, lying, risk-taking. For those not so afflicted it seems inexplicable that otherwise righteous, committed Latter-day Saints could be afflicted with such problems, yet it is not uncommon.

At the root of all such problems is anxiety. For reasons that lie buried in their personal histories, these people are subject to recurring bouts of severe anxiety. Often their ultimate fear is that they will be abandoned by everyone they love. Perhaps they have had actual experience as a young child with such abandonment or other traumatic events. In any case, at some point they learned to associate some particular behavior with the release of this tension. Sex, of course, relieves tension, and it is not too surprising that some people adopt sexual fantasies and behaviors as their way of dealing with these pressures.

This kind of emotional problem requires the help of an experienced therapist. Typically, the counselor works first on the sources of the anxiety that overwhelms these people and overshadows the promises they have made to themselves and others not to indulge in these hurtful and humiliating practices. Then, when some progress has been made in defusing the anxiety, strategies for eliminating the symptom may be discussed.

The reverse order will simply never work, as thousands who have tried it will testify. But it is important to assure discouraged victims of this type of illness that it does yield to professionally directed effort. Although the temptation may continue, effective means for reducing and managing the anxiety can provide permanent control over the symptom. Those who have suffered the shame and humiliation of such an affliction compare this achievement to being freed from bondage. Their spouses are scarcely less appreciative.

The third category of special difficulty comprises couples who, for a variety of reasons, are not able to function sexually in the normal way. Such couples feel particular emotional pain in their handicap, not only for themselves but also for their "cheated" partner. Some have felt particularly bitter because local priesthood leaders have been unbending in forbidding alternative forms of lovemaking that are possible to them but are felt to be "unnatural." I do not challenge the guidelines set forth by local priesthood authorities. I do, however, counsel such couples that the Lord has given couples responsibility over this part of their lives. They are the ones who need to seek inspiration about what is appropriate for their special circumstances. I am reminded that in the temple, where everything must be absolutely correctly done, the Lord has nevertheless compassionately provided for the person who lacks one hand to use the other, who lacks a right foot to use the left foot, who lacks both hands and both feet to nevertheless be accommodated. This gives me the courage to extend the hope that a couple might take their special problem to the Lord and obtain a compassionate response from him.

It is my conviction that every couple in any circumstance has the opportunity and obligation to fill the measure of their creation and find joy in doing so, in this as well as in every other part of their lives together.

God has said that it is not good for man to be alone. It is his commandment that a man and woman become one flesh. It should not be surprising that when we pursue that relationship following the principles that inspired leaders have outlined, the result is a unique bonding, an ennobling loyalty, and a glow that partakes of the divine.

CHAPTER 2

"FORSAKING ALL OTHERS"

One of the most satisfying rewards of a good marriage is the sense of being the most important person in the world to one other person. This feeling is so basic that it was mentioned in one of only two observations about the nature of marriage that Adam made when God presented him with a wife. In addition to noting that they would be one flesh, Adam declared: "Therefore shall a man leave his father and his mother, and shall cleave unto his wife." (Genesis 2:24.)

In this observation Adam not only established the principle that this relationship should be primary above all other mortal relationships, but he also indicated that it was important to set a new boundary between the couple and their relatives. The point is not, of course, that parents are the sole challengers for the first loyalty of the partners. We will consider a variety of other competitors. But from Adam forward it has been recognized that often enough it is relatives who are the sometimes unintended saboteurs of the marital bond. Since, as a people, we value and promote strong family ties, it is hard to accept the fact that if such ties are not limited and disciplined after the wedding they can and will strangle a marriage. Two modern apostles have made the point as well as anyone could.

President Hugh B. Brown has written, "As each new marriage craft sets sail, there should be a warning call, which is familiar to all ocean travelers, 'All ashore that's going ashore,' whereupon all in-laws should get off the matrimonial boat and return only at infrequent intervals and then only as invited guests for brief visits." (Hugh B. Brown, *You and Your Marriage* [Salt Lake City: Bookcraft, 1960], p. 138.)

Elder Boyd K. Packer, has, if possible, stated the case even more strongly. First among the instructions he gives couples whom he is asked to seal in the temple is the following admonition: "First of all, today, as you are sealed for time and for all eternity, you become a separate family on the records of the Church, and that is a separation in a very real sense. All of the ties that have bound you to your father and mother to this point we undo today. We untie them all. . . . Many of them we leave permanently untied. That is why your mothers will be crying today . . . because they know, in a very real sense, that they are losing and that they should lose you as you become a separate family on the records of the Church." (Boyd K. Packer, *That All May Be Edified* [Salt Lake City: Bookcraft, 1982], pp. 226-27.)

Often there are circumstances that make this separation especially difficult. Perhaps the husband's mother is widowed and dependent on him for emotional and practical support; or the husband may work for his family or his wife's family so that the couple's affairs are almost inextricably intertwined with the "in-laws"; or the couple may be financially or otherwise obligated to one of the families; or one or more of the in-laws may be particularly demanding or intrusive.

The problem may be part of a larger complex of problems. I think of an Idaho farm girl who had grown up as part of a warm, expressive extended family, attended Brigham Young University, and married a returned missionary who was about to graduate in engineering. He got a job in the aerospace industry in Los Angeles, and settled her in a small apartment in, to her, a frightening urban neighborhood. He worked long hours on various projects that always seemed to be on emergency status and to require extraordinary amounts of time and energy. She found their new ward cold, and she spent much of her time alone in her crowded apartment crying her heart out. Her one release was to call her mother in Idaho, and the husband soon discovered that she was running up telephone bills that were as high as the rent. When summer came, she insisted they return to Idaho for their vacation. She loved the trip and felt like a fish out of water returning to her native lake. He felt very much the outsider and spent most of his time alone or sleeping since he didn't know how to join in her family's conversations, which were full of people and places and events he had never heard of and had no interest in. At the end of two weeks he had to return to work. She refused to go with him, staying the rest of the summer with her family. In fact, it was with the greatest difficulty that she was persuaded to rejoin him in the fall. When she did, she spent most of their time together complaining about Los Angeles and pressuring him to find some kind of a job in Idaho. He replied that in his business there were no jobs in Idaho, that Los Angeles was where they could expect to live for the rest of his career and that she might as well grow up and get used to it.

By the time I saw them a year later she had had a baby, which had, if possible, redoubled her determination to move back to Idaho. No way was she going to raise her baby in that awful city environment. She gave an ultimatum: either they move as a family to Idaho, even if it meant giving up his work as an engineer and getting into some other kind of employment, or she and the baby would go alone and he could stay in Los Angeles by himself.

It is easy to label this young mother as immature and disloyal and to point to the generations of women who have courageously done what they had to do, often in circumstances more challenging than hers, without complaint or threat. In fact, if I am not mistaken, on the couple's first visit with me, I read to the wife the scriptural passage about leaving father and mother and cleaving to her husband, but she snapped back that she had had that quoted to her until she never wanted to hear it again, that people didn't understand that she couldn't *stand* it in Los Angeles, and that the prospect of staying the rest of her life and raising her family in such inhospitable surroundings was beyond her capacity to cope with. Better to return to the good people who loved her and to the clean air and wholesome conditions of her native countryside as a single mother than to stay here as a wife ("if you can even call it that . . . he's never home").

It was clear that her own immaturity was aggravated by her husband's having failed to keep *his* priorities straight. Absorbed in his exciting and demanding new job, he had virtually abandoned his young family in this inhospitable environment. After some discussion, we agreed that she would stay for at least six more months if he would rearrange his life to give time for his family and also find better living quarters in a better neighborhood and in a warmer ward. He also began to see the importance of being more supportive of her in general, and she discovered that this was much easier for him to do if she quit complaining about everything all the time. (He confessed at one point that he had sometimes worked late when he didn't have to because he hated to come home to listen to her dissatisfactions every evening.)

At the end of six months she and her husband had rediscovered the reasons they had married in the first place. She had settled into her new home and ward and had voluntarily cut her calls to her family in Idaho to one a week. In the final session we had together, she said, "I cannot believe how immaturely and selfishly I was behaving when we first came in." Yet, in fairness to her, her difficulty in putting her husband first in her life had been only the mirror image of his difficulty in putting her first in his.

The fact of the matter is that it is not only in-laws who may challenge the primacy of the marital commitment. In this case, the husband's job had been placed above his wife and her needs. In other cases, the problem may be friends, the children, or hobbies. Even Church responsibilities can subvert proper attention to a spouse and family.

One young bishop's wife spoke for many "Church widows" and "widowers" when she said, "I love you and I try to support you in your calling, but I resent being number 22 on your list." He replied that it was ridiculous for her to feel that way, and that in any case if she knew as much about the marriages in the ward as he did, she would be forced to acknowledge that "number 22 on my list is a lot better off than number 1 on most other husbands' lists." He was taken aback when she replied, "Maybe so, but often I think I would rather be number 1 on somebody else's list."

As we discussed the issues in this marriage, it became clear that the amount of time he spent with his family was not the issue. She was prepared to sacrifice time together so that he could perform his Church duties; but she could only do so cheerfully if he communicated to her in convincing ways that she was still the most important person in his life. Instead, he unwittingly conveyed the impression that she was an "also ran" in his life. For example, he would promise to take her out but would often permit last-minute ward emergencies to interfere. "I may have the world's foremost collection of 'rain checks,' " she said. Even their anniversaries were not sacred but had, on several occasions, been sacrificed to some more pressing ward or stake business. "Honey, I *have* to be there," he would explain. "I'm the bishop."

I had to explain to this good man that his wife would never believe that she was the most important person in his life until he showed that he was willing to defend commitments to her against all comers. She agreed that their dates could be relatively far apart, but she needed to be able to *count* on them. Also, she needed to have their dates unencumbered with other obligations. When they did go out together it was not uncommon for him to work in a few errands on the way to wherever they were going. "This'll just take a minute, Honey," he would say as he left her in the car while he dropped off a few things at the Relief Society president's place or stopped by the home of the chairman of the Activities Committee to sign a couple of checks. It was not easy, at first, for him to see the importance of excluding all such distractions from their time together. She was hungry for indications that he was thinking of her while he was away from her (the unexpected phone call home or note or gift) rather than that he was thinking of other things when he was with her. He had to learn that it was not inappropriate or unreasonable of her to expect *evidence* that she was indeed number one in his life.

This principle is true for both partners. For example, when

a woman becomes pregnant and then brings a new child into the world, she may become so focused on all of the exciting and draining demands of her new role that all couple-oriented activities simply lapse. Studies have shown that the only couples who do not suffer in their relationships during the childbearing years of their marriage are those who plan for and rigorously protect their time and activities together. The crucial element seems not to be the absolute frequency (although the pillars need to be close enough together to hold up the roof) but the absolute certainty that the time will be protected because the *marriage* is important to each.

The gospel principle involved here is one of the most basic of all, the law of the harvest. As a man or woman soweth, so also shall he or she reap. Marriages are living things. If they are cultivated and nourished, they will thrive. If they are neglected, they will wither and sometimes die.

But as sensible a reason as that is for fostering one's marriage, for those sealed in the House of the Lord there is a more compelling reason. I had this brought home to me when a couple who were good friends came to me for counseling and a blessing. They were fine Latter-day Saints who loved the Lord. They loved their children, too, but they had mixed feelings toward each other. Over the twenty years of their marriage, she had found him passive and resistant to her suggestions. When things got tough, his strategy was to withdraw and leave her to handle things. He, on the other hand, complained that she found fault with him continually and never showed appreciation for his contributions to the family. Each admitted that there was some truth in the other's complaint but declared themselves to be just too emotionally exhausted to cope with each other anymore. He was over his head in a business crisis and stated flatly that he lacked the energy to deal with his wife, so he had left home and moved in with a friend. She reported that she had just about reached bottom and had considered taking her own life. Each sat in a pool of discouragement and stubborn self-pity. Divorce was one of the alternatives they were considering.

My usual manner toward people in emotional pain is to be

empathic and gentle and to help them feel accepted and understood. This generally works much better than giving advice, since nearly everyone who comes to see me knows perfectly well what they should do, and a little warmth and understanding gives them the strength to get to work on it.

But in this case the Lord took the issue out of my hands. I was prompted by the Spirit to remind the couple that they were *not* released from their responsibility for the marriage because they were weary and discouraged. It was unacceptable to the Lord that they offer *any* excuse for not doing the things that they knew perfectly well they must do in order to make their marriage work. In the blessing that followed, I heard myself telling the husband that he was like a reluctant Jonah, attempting to flee from his Nineveh. He was reminded that he had made no eternal covenants with his business associates or lawyers or bankers, but that before God and authoritative witnesses he had taken a most holy oath to be the husband of this woman and to shepherd her and his children born under that covenant back to the kingdom. He was told that in the Lord's eyes, this was by far his most serious stewardship. For this purpose he had come to this earth. His eternal salvation depended on his faithful fulfillment of that duty. His business was only a means of supporting his material needs, and the Lord would not abandon him in that if he gave priority to the things that deserved his full energy and commitment.

At the end of that blessing, all three of us were in tears, and I as well as they had learned the Lord's perspective on the significance of a temple marriage. I do not know if this couple will heed the warning the Lord gave. I know that in their place I would heed it as though my eternal salvation depended upon it, as indeed it does. In fact, I have urgently reviewed my own priorities to make sure that my own house is in order in this matter.

The Lord has said: "Thou shalt love thy wife with all thy heart, and shalt cleave unto her and none else." (D&C 42:22.) He has also said that we are not to "commit adultery . . . nor do anything like unto it." (D&C 59:6.) One of the most important provisions of the marital covenant is that each partner will restrict his or her romantic and sexual involvement to the other. There is safety and satisfaction in this assurance. Few marital tragedies are more disruptive than the violation of the covenant of fidelity.

When I was a young branch president in Athens, Georgia, Elder Spencer W. Kimball, at that time a member of the Twelve, visited our stake as a conference visitor. About a week before the conference, each bishop and branch president got a letter inviting us to a Saturday afternoon meeting with Elder Kimball. Our Relief Society presidents were also invited to a separate meeting at the same hour. But the letter went on to say that Elder Kimball had specifically requested that the priesthood leaders and Relief Society presidents *not* travel together to the meeting unless accompanied by at least one of their spouses. Frankly, I was offended at the implication that I couldn't travel seventy miles in broad daylight with my Relief Society president (who, incidentally,was twice my age) without getting into some sort of trouble. Moreover, this placed us in a real dilemma as to how to arrange our joint attendance at the meeting. My wife and I had three children under the age of four, and while we had just about got up our nerve to take the whole crew to Atlanta for the Sunday morning session of conference, there was no way in the world that I could expect her to take them also on Saturday just to chaperone Sister Turner and me. Sister Turner's husband was a tile setter who had to work six days a week just to keep bread on his family's table. I couldn't very well ask him to get off work to keep an eye on us. And it just seemed ridiculous to drive two cars seventy miles to Atlanta and seventy miles back because somebody in Salt Lake City didn't think we could make it in one car without being morally corrupted. Fortunately, my second counselor and his wife, hearing of our problem, volunteered to take us and do a little shopping while we were in our meetings. This seemed to me to meet the spirit if not the exact letter of the law, so I took them up on it.

At the meeting, Elder Kimball, after some opening remarks, announced that the rest of the time would be devoted to answering any questions we might have. No one raised their hands for a few moments. So, twenty-five years old and brash, I raised mine. "Yes, President Broderick?" (He remembered my name from the introductions at the beginning of the meeting. I was impressed but undeterred.)

"Elder Kimball, could you explain to us how it is that you brethren trust us enough to call us as priesthood leaders and Relief Society presidents but not enough to drive together unchaperoned to a Church meeting?"

He looked at me mildly over his glasses. "Is it your thought then, President, that we just sit in Salt Lake City and make up these rules?"

I could sense that somehow I had lost the initiative in the exchange. I replied, "Well, I guess so, more or less."

"Oh, no," he said gravely, "we came to that rule only after we had lost a few bishops and Relief Society presidents."

"In the *Church?*" I blurted.

He just smiled sadly at me and asked for the next question.

It had never occurred to me that such a thing could happen. Since then I have had the sad duty of sitting on courts for seminary teachers, quorum presidents, members of bishoprics, and high councilors. No one is secure simply by virtue of his or her Church calling.

In the process of counseling couples, both in and out of the Church, I have learned many things I would never have guessed about the why's and how's and who's of adultery. For one thing, I have become persuaded that people's virtues as well as their vices may play an important part in their infidelity.

I think for example of a young stake missionary. He had a temple marriage and was widely looked up to as intensely spiritual. He was effective in his calling and seemed quite unafraid to talk to anyone about the gospel. Most people showed no interest, but he was gratified to sense in his secretary (a young divorcée, still dazed by the painful breakup of her marriage) a sincere interest in making some sense out of her shattered life. When time permitted, they would get into deep gospel conversations, and gradually he drew from her the story of her unhappy childhood, youth, and marriage. His heart ached for her. He told her that her Heavenly Father loved her and had sent her to her job to learn of the gospel of Jesus Christ and be healed. Often, so that they could discuss these important matters without interruption or rude comments from other staff members, they would take long lunches together, and on several occasions he stopped off at her apartment to continue a discussion begun at work. His wife grew increasingly disconcerted at his late homecomings. He was disappointed that she did not feel that the value of a soul was greater than her convenience. In order to demonstrate to this golden contact (he called her his "Little Goldie") that God loved her and that *he* loved her, he began giving her a reassuring hug when he left her. She was very appreciative of his compassion and saw him almost as her savior. On one occasion when he hugged her, she pulled him to her and kissed him. He was overwhelmed by the flood of feelings that washed over him, and before that visit was ended he had violated his covenants.

By the time he confessed his sin to his wife and stake president a few weeks later, he was convinced that he loved this woman as he had never loved his wife, and that she and her two young sons needed him more than his own family did. He promised her that after he had divorced his wife and paid the penalty for his sin, he would yet baptize her and take her to the temple. Clear through the Church court, he insisted that although he had been wrong to violate his temple vows, he had been sent to this young woman by God.

It is difficult to say at exactly what point this man's spiritual pride, ability to rationalize, and poor judgment combined to lead him from righteous sharing of the gospel to unrighteous indulgence and betrayal of his marital vows. Certainly it was early in the relationship. But he was so bemused by the virtue of his own motivation and by the intensity of the "spirit" he felt when with his "Little Goldie" that he was immune to warnings from his wife, his friends, or even the Spirit. From the beginning he should have involved his wife in proselyting his investigator or referred her to the full-time missionaries. There are reasons for such "stuffy" rules, and he eventually discovered all of them.

I am impressed over and over again with how easily some Latter-day Saints permit themselves to get into potentially destructive situations because they know that only *good* people are involved and that the love they feel is pure and "special." I am particularly impressed with the frequency with which they claim that they felt the "Spirit" guiding them. I have come to call these "hormonal revelations" and am reminded of my oldest daughter's first vacation home after attending Brigham Young University. "Daddy, Daddy," she cried as she ran to give me a hug, "guess what. *Eight* boys had it revealed to them that they were to marry me, and that's more than any other girl on our floor."

This same spirit seems also to influence married adults, who have more cause to have developed common sense and the spirit of discernment. The following case is typical of many that end in the destruction of Latter-day Saint families.

Don and Shirley were married in the temple and had two young children. Their closest friends were Paul and Carol. The wives took turns babysitting for each other and were visiting with each other by phone or in person every day. The men played handball together and occasionally went to sports events together when their wives didn't want to go. But most of all they loved to do things together as couples. Every month they went to the temple together. One winter they rented a condominium at a ski resort and went skiing together. For a while they all jogged together, but then Carol got pregnant and dropped out and Don pulled a leg muscle. Don was glad, however, that Paul was still running with Shirley, because he would worry if she had to run alone in these troubled times when anything might happen.

The two surviving joggers came to look forward to their early morning rendezvous as the best part of the day. They could not have said when they realized that their feelings for each other began to exceed their feelings for their spouses. Gradually they came to believe that they had been promised to each other in the premortal existence. When their spouses began to become uneasy at the amount of time they were spending together, they insisted that they were no more than friends and that they were disappointed in the lack of trust their spouses displayed. Eventually both families were destroyed.

Again we see the working of spiritual pride, rationalization, and bad judgment. Because these good people did not set out to commit adultery, they refused to recognize the signs that they were approaching that unhappy sin and disdained the sacrifice of each other's company that could have prevented it.

For myself, my temple vows are of sufficient importance to me that I avoid even the entrances to the paths that lead in that direction. Some think me too cautious, but much is at stake, and a little ridicule never hurt anyone.

In sum, we are counseled by the Lord that "Thou shalt love thy wife with all thy heart, and shalt cleave unto her and none else." (D&C 42:22.) "None else," as we have seen, includes relatives and friends and the children and "golden contacts." It includes one's work, one's hobbies, television, and one's Church callings. Specifically and explicitly included in "none else" are members of the opposite (or same) sex who threaten one's emotional and sexual loyalty. In the scripture cited above, the Lord goes on to say, "And he that looketh upon a woman to lust after her shall deny the faith, and shall not have the Spirit; and if he repents not he shall be cast out." (D&C 42:23.) I bear sad, solemn witness that this is so.

CHAPTER 3

"WITHOUT COMPULSORY MEANS"

As a result of her transgression in the garden of Eden, Eve was given a double burden. First, God told her, "I will greatly multiply thy sorrow and thy conception; in sorrow thou shalt bring forth children." Then he added, "and thy desire shall be to thy husband, and he shall rule over thee." (Genesis 3:16.) Women have debated ever since which of the two burdens is the worst, for the simple truth is that most men have not mastered the principle of governing their family in the Lord's own way. The problem does not, I believe, lie in a lack of guidance from the Lord on the matter. The principles are very clearly laid out in the scriptures. Despite this, there remains a great deal of confusion, even among good Latter-day Saints, as to how to be a righteous patriarch and how to be the eternal partner of one.

As I work with families in the Church, sometimes it seems to me that most of them can be divided into two equally problematic leadership styles. In one group the father and husband is very insistent that his patriarchal rights be honored. Should his wife ever challenge one of his opinions or demands, he quickly reminds her of her temple vows and calls on her to repent and support the priesthood authority in her home. Any degree of rebellion on the part of the children is met with the declaration that the father is appointed by God to preside in his home as the Prophet is appointed to preside over the Church, and that to defy either is tantamount to apostasy. This style often leads to the very rebellion from wife and children that it seeks to suppress. Alternatively, it may lead to an overly submissive, dependent, and depressed wife and children. In their striving to be strong, worthy leaders in their homes, these husbands have slipped across the line from righteous to unrighteous dominion.

The second and larger group of families fall into the style of leadership that I call "patriarchy from the rear." In these families the wife is the one earnestly seeking to establish a proper patriarchal relationship in the home. Her husband, however, lacks the vision or the commitment necessary to fulfill his role so that she ends up constantly "encouraging" (he would say nagging) him to take his place as the spiritual leader of the family. Gradually her list of disappointments grows. He doesn't lead in family prayer; he takes no responsibility to structure family scripture reading or family home evening. He never interviews the children, and if it were left to him to organize things, the couple would never get to the temple or, for that matter, go out together on regular dates. In fact, he puts off his home teaching and other responsibilities to the last minute and often wouldn't get them done at all if she didn't prod and push and carry on about it. She *hates* the role of prime mover she has assumed. When she married a returned missionary, she assumed that he would be the leader, and she is bitterly resentful that he is not.

As one sister put it, "One time I purposely refused to take the lead in organizing family prayer or family home evening just to see how long he would let it lapse before he picked up the responsibility. After four weeks I finally gave up. If it were up to him we would *never* have those things."

On the husband's side there is also bitterness and resentment. Sometimes it is up front: "Get off my case!" More often it is passively expressed by postponing, forgetting, and making excuses. There may be promises and apologies, but rarely performance. When pushed to express their feelings directly, these reluctant patriarchs confess that they feel they could never meet their wives' expectations anyway, so why try; no matter what they did, it wouldn't be enough. The wives often feed this fear by being critical of any effort their husbands do make, seeing it as too little, too late, and not sufficiently self-motivated.

It seems to me that both groups of families miss the mark. For one thing, all doctrinal considerations aside, neither style of leadership works well. Each, however well-intentioned, leaves a residue of resentment and rebellion. Each, whether purposely or not, attempts to impose a degree of compulsion that, in the long run, simply never succeeds.

President Gordon B. Hinckley addressed these issues in a couples' fireside beamed by satellite to the whole Church on January 29, 1984. He said, in part:

> To men within the sound of my voice, wherever you may be, I say, if you are guilty of demeaning behavior toward your wife, if you are prone to dictate and exercise authority over her, if you are selfish and brutal in your actions in the home, then stop it! Repent! Repent now while you have the opportunity to do so.
>
> To you wives who are constantly complaining and see only the dark side of life, and feel that you are unloved and unwanted, look into your own hearts and minds. If there is something wrong, turn about. Put a smile on your faces. Make yourselves attractive. Brighten your outlook. You deny yourselves happiness and court misery if you constantly complain and do nothing to rectify your own faults. Rise above the shrill clamor over rights and prerogatives, and walk in the quiet dignity of a daughter of God.

The scriptures spell out three principles that must be observed if the blessings of smooth, satisfying family relations are to be enjoyed. First is the principle of order; second is the principle of unity; and third is the principle of agency. The three are so intertwined in the marital relationship that it is difficult to discuss any one of them without bringing in the other two; nevertheless, it is useful to look at the unique contribution of each to a harmonious marriage.

The Principle of Order

The marital union is not simply a relationship between a man and a woman; it is intended to be the leadership coalition of a family enterprise. The Lord has assigned to this unit several grave and important tasks, among which is the task of raising up children unto him. The relationship of husband and wife can be properly understood only in the light of the assignments given to them. The Lord's perspective on this is vividly and pointedly expressed in the revelation given in section 93 of the Doctrine and Covenants. The first half of the revelation is a remarkable outline of the nature and purpose of man. In that context the Lord saw fit to bring the general doctrine down to its most practical application and called the three members of the First Presidency (Joseph Smith, Sidney Rigdon, and Frederick G. Williams) and the highest local authority (Bishop Newel K. Whitney) to repent of their negligence in performing their patriarchal responsibilities and to put their houses in order. It is worth pondering the pertinent passages from the Doctrine and Covenants:

> The glory of God is intelligence, or, in other words, light and truth. Light and truth forsake that evil one. Every spirit of man was innocent in the beginning; and God having redeemed man from the fall, men became again, in their infant state, innocent before God. And that wicked one cometh and taketh away light and truth, through disobedience, from the children of men, and because of the tradition of their fathers.
>
> But I have commanded you to bring up your children in light and truth. But verily I say unto you, my servant Frederick G. Williams, you have continued under this condemnation; you have not taught your children light and truth, according to the commandments; and that wicked one hath power, as yet, over you, and this is the cause of your affliction.
>
> And now a commandment I give unto you—if you will be delivered you shall set in order your own house, for there are many things that are not right in your house.
>
> Verily, I say unto my servant Sidney Rigdon, that in some things he hath not kept the commandments concerning his children; therefore, first set in order thy house. . . .
>
> And now, verily I say unto Joseph Smith, Jun.—you have not kept the commandments, and must needs stand rebuked before the Lord; your family must needs repent and forsake some things, and give more earnest heed unto your sayings, or be removed out of their place.
>
> What I say unto one I say unto all; pray always lest that

26

wicked one have power in you, and remove you out of your place.

My servant Newel K. Whitney also, a bishop of my church, hath need to be chastened, and set in order his family, and see that they are more diligent and concerned at home, and pray always, or they shall be removed out of their place. (D&C 93:36-50.)

My hunch is that these brethren were surprised and perhaps offended to be the ones called down on this matter. Why didn't the Lord address this rebuke to their wives? After all, these men were working night and day for the Church and trying to support their families at the same time. Their wives had by far the greatest involvement in the upbringing of their children. Why did the Lord come down so hard on the fathers?

Apparently, it is the Lord's view that the priesthood is given to men not just to bless and teach the Church at large but to bless and teach their families. These brethren were chastised because they were neglecting a crucial part of their priesthood responsibility. In the kingdom there is no place for disengaged or disinterested fathers who leave all of the childrearing to their wives. Husbands are to be active rather than absent or passive partners to their wives in these matters. Part of what it means to have your home *in order* is to have the patriarch *in place* at the head of the family.

I have discovered this over and over as a family therapist. It is not uncommon for a family to come in to see me that has a strong, hard-working, psychologically minded woman at its heart and a weak or abusive or disengaged husband at its periphery. Nearly always they are having trouble with one or more of the children. It is perfectly clear (at least to me and to the wife) that one of the problems is that the father is not playing his part well. The temptation, of course, is to become the substitute patriarch in this family, joining with the wife in setting the family's affairs in order. In such a plan, the father is either ignored or treated as one of the children who has to be reeducated on how to behave in the family circle. Frequently, he drops out of counseling after only a few sessions. In my experience this approach virtually never works. When

I am successful in family therapy, it is because I have been wise enough to assign the father the task of finding the solution to the family's problems—no matter how wrong-headed or distant or irresponsible he may be.

I remember a family in which both parents were active but all five children had been "lost." The mother was a sensitive, self-educated woman who attended every Brigham Young University Education Week and read everything in the Church bookstore on how to raise a family. But her husband was a rough-cut man who got along well enough with most of the men in the ward but was ignorant of most principles of human relationships or communication. He had been physically abused as a child and had physically abused all five of his children. His four sons had run away from home as soon as they got old enough to find anywhere to run to. His youngest child, a daughter, had stayed home but became openly promiscuous despite the beatings and other coercive tactics employed to curb her immoral behavior. In the midst of all this the mother had a nervous breakdown. On a bishop's referral I saw her in therapy, and then her daughter; but the father refused to come in, feeling that counseling was a "bunch of psychological garbage." However, when he learned that I was also a stake president, he agreed to come in once with his wife for a consultation on how to help his daughter straighten out her life.

As soon as they sat down in my office the wife started to lecture him through me: "Doctor Broderick, don't you think that we'd have better luck with Janice if we let up a little on her? I was so impressed with the point you made in your book about 'emotional space.' "

I could see that the husband was feeling he had been ambushed (as indeed he had). His jaw was getting firmer and his body tenser. I interrupted his wife long enough to say, "Brother Jensen, you don't get much respect in your family, do you?"

He looked at me sharply, wondering perhaps how I had figured that out. Then he looked down at his shoes and mumbled, "Not much."

His wife said, "Karl, how can you say that? You're an absolute tyrant at home. We do everything to try to please you."

He turned to her and said, "You think I don't know you're always on the phone with the boys [their runaway sons, then young adults living very worldly life-styles] after I've told you not to have nothing to do with them after all the pain they caused us? You think I don't know you sneak food up to Janice after I send her to bed without no dinner? You never respected me!"

"Well, I respect you," I said. "You are the head of your family, and neither I nor your wife have the keys of revelation for that Church unit. You do. So, what should we do to help Janice?"

His wife looked at me as though I had lost my marbles.

He said, "We've tried everything. Nothing works with that girl. I even locked her in her room, and last week I found out she's climbing out the window and shimmying down the rain spout after we're in bed."

I said, "Well, if you can't think of anything right now, why don't you go home and pray about it and come back next week and tell us how we should proceed. If this is going to work out, it will have to be in the Lord's way, and that is with you as head of your family."

He looked hard at his wife, then back at me, and said, "Okay, I'll pray about it," and got up to leave.

She said, "Dear, you go on out to the car. I want to stay a minute and talk to Dr. Broderick about a couple of things."

I said, "No, let's wait till next week and see what the Lord and your husband come up with," and I walked with them to the parking lot.

The next week's session started as the first week's had, with her trying to teach him correct principles through me, but as soon as I could get a word in I said to him, "Well, what did you come up with?"

He said, "I wondered if you'd remembered. Well, I got that we ought to have her read her patriarchal blessing."

That was not a very creative idea. They had been trying to get her to pray with the family and read her patriarchal blessing and the like for months without effect. The wife rolled her eyes to the ceiling and groaned. "Great idea," I said. "Try it and see what happens."

What happened was what had happened every other time they had tried it: the girl refused. "She wouldn't do it," he said when they came in the next week.

"Of course she wouldn't do it," his wife said. "I've told you over and over you can't just cram religion down her throat. Just last month I heard a talk on that at Education Week—"

"So," I interrupted, "what's next?"

"I don't know," he said, "I got she should read her patriarchal blessing and she wouldn't, so I guess we're stuck."

"Oh, I'm sure the Lord has more than one arrow in his quiver," I said. "If she had read her blessing, as you suggested, it doubtless would have been helpful, but she wouldn't, so you must go back to the Lord and find out what to do next."

The next week he came back and said, "I got I should walk and talk with her."

"Beg pardon?" I said.

"Walk and talk with her," he repeated.

Now this man had *never* walked or talked or anything like unto it with any of his five children. He was more of a yeller and hitter. So it was with some nervousness that I said, "Great! That's a wonderful idea. You walk and talk with her this week."

As it happened, I was seeing the daughter later that afternoon, and I told her what had happened. She said, "Walk and talk with me? That's not his style. He'll never do it."

"Oh, he'll do it," I said. "He may not do it well, because he doesn't know how, but I'll kick you around the block [I knew her well enough to tease her in this language] if you make it hard for him."

"Why would I make it hard for him?" she asked, her eyes tearing up for the first time since I had known her. "My dad has never cared enough about me to walk and talk with me in my life, and he won't do it now either."

But he did. When she came home that evening, he grabbed her by the elbow, dragged her out in the backyard, and said, "I need to walk and talk with you." After a few minutes of marching her around the yard and telling her how much she meant to him and how it hurt him to see her throw herself away, he stopped and said, "I think I'm supposed to listen, too," and they marched around some more while she tried to put her feelings into words.

Within six weeks they had become the best of friends (somewhat to the mother's chagrin), but the best part was that one day Janice told me, "Nobody in the world could have convinced me that my daddy could change, but he has. And if he could change, anybody could change. Maybe there's even hope for me."

I have had many such experiences. My conclusion is that there is no family strategy that is so likely to work as the father's exercising righteous patriarchal initiative to "put his house in order."

To summarize, the principle of order requires that the patriarch function in his family as the priesthood leader in his home. Without the other two principles discussed in this chapter, however (the principle of unity and the principle of agency), patriarchy can turn into its ugly counterfeit, tyranny.

The Principle of Unity

Immediately after setting me apart as a stake president, Elder Boyd K. Packer sat me down to give me a few points of advice on how to succeed in my new calling. I was fully prepared to be receptive to his counsel, but I couldn't help being taken aback by his first admonition.

"Now, President, I don't want you treating your wife like you do the stake."

I was mildly offended. I said, "I wasn't planning on treating either the stake or my wife badly."

"I know," he continued, "but you need to treat them well, differently. In the stake when a decision is to be made, you will seek the opinion of your counselors and other concerned individuals. Then you will prayerfully reach a decision on the matter, and they will all rally round and support you because you are the president and you have the mantle of authority.

In your family when there is a decision to be made that affects everyone, you and your wife together will seek whatever counsel you might need, and together you will prayerfully come to a unified decision. If you ever pull priesthood rank on her you will have failed in your leadership."

I have thought a lot about that, and I believe it is true. In fact, I took that as the goal for my presidency also. We made all our decisions in the unity of the Spirit, and I virtually never had to "pull rank" on my counselors.

When Paul compared the unity between a husband and wife to the unity between Christ and the Church, he set a high standard for that holy union. After affirming the principle of order, he continued:

> Husbands, love your wives, even as Christ also loved the church, and gave himself for it; that he might sanctify and cleanse it with the washing of water by the word, that he might present it to himself a glorious church, not having spot, or wrinkle, or any such thing; but that it should be holy and without blemish. So ought men to love their wives as their own bodies.
>
> He that loveth his wife loveth himself. For no man ever yet hated his own flesh; but nourisheth and cherisheth it, even as the Lord the church: for we are members of his body, of his flesh, and of his bones. For this cause shall a man leave his father and mother, and shall be joined unto his wife, and they two shall be one flesh. This is a great mystery: but I speak concerning Christ and the church. Nevertheless let every one of you in particular so love his wife even as himself; and the wife see that she reverence her husband. (Ephesians 5:25-33.)

Elsewhere the Lord has said to the Church (and presumably to every unit in it, including the family unit): "Be kindly affectioned one to another with brotherly love; in honour preferring one another.... Be of the same mind one toward another." (Romans 12:10, 16.)

The Lord has also said: "I say unto you, be one; and if ye are not one ye are not mine." (D&C 38:27.)

In the family that practices the principle of unity, the principle of order never chafes. But there is yet another principle that rounds out our understanding of the nature of decision-making and governance in celestial unions, the principle of agency.

The Principle of Agency

There is an old saying that you can lead a horse to water but you can't make him drink. To me this is nothing more nor less than a homespun restatement of the principle of agency. Not only *should* we respect each other's agency, it is not really possible to destroy another's agency. But we try; we try.

I refer not only to patriarchal tyrants who attempt to impose their will upon their families, but also to wives who attempt to do the same thing in the name of righteousness. When I point out to these usually well-motivated and sincere people that they are violating the letter and spirit of the charter for the legitimate exercise of righteous authority spelled out in section 121 of the Doctrine and Covenants, they sometimes counter with verse 37, which says that "to exercise control or dominion or compulsion upon the souls of the children of men, *in any degree of unrighteousness,* " is condemned. (Italics added.) In their own case, they insist that the attempt to exercise "control or dominion or compulsion" is righteously motivated, and they often challenge me to fault the virtue of their goals. Their view seems to be that compulsory means are justified if the ends are worthy.

In this as in other cases it is wise to read the whole scripture. The chapter goes on to say:

> No power or influence can or ought to be maintained by virtue of the priesthood, only by persuasion, by long-suffering, by gentleness and meekness, and by love unfeigned; by kindness, and pure knowledge, which shall greatly enlarge the soul without hypocrisy, and without guile—reproving betimes with sharpness, when moved upon by the Holy Ghost; and then showing forth afterwards an increase of love toward him whom thou hast reproved, lest he esteem thee to be his enemy; that he may know that thy faithfulness is stronger than the cords of death.
>
> Let thy bowels also be full of charity towards all men, and to the household of faith, and let virtue garnish thy thoughts

unceasingly; then shall thy confidence wax strong in the presence of God; and the doctrine of the priesthood shall distil upon thy soul as the dews from heaven. The Holy Ghost shall be thy constant companion, and thy scepter an unchanging scepter of righteousness and truth; and thy dominion shall be an everlasting dominion, *and without compulsory means* it shall flow unto thee forever and ever. (D&C 121:41-46; italics added.)

One day a young woman came into my office to protest the idea of patriarchal leadership in the home. She felt that such an idea gave her second-class status in the kingdom, and she had no intention of being "ruled over" by her husband. She was a recently married convert to the Church and was a very bright, independent, modern woman. She was confident that her judgment was at least as good as her husband's, and she could see no reason to defer to him or his ideas. She had a point; actually I felt that her husband was a shade "light-weight," if I may use the term, and that I would personally have valued her opinion over his on most things.

But I pointed out to her that I too had, on one or two occasions, felt that I was presided over by a bishop or quorum leader who was not as well grounded in either good judgment or gospel principles as I, but in each case I sustained him in his office. This had never required me to give up my free agency or to abandon my own resources of experience and wisdom.

Moreover, the only authority they had toward me, according to the Doctrine and Covenants, was to preside through meek and gentle long-suffering with unpretended love toward me. They were authorized to be kind to me and to seek and share pure knowledge from God on my behalf. It was permitted them to call me to repentance if they perceived through the Holy Spirit that I was straying off the path; but they were then obligated to show me even greater concern and affection lest I be offended by their warning.

I asked her if that kind of leadership would upset her. She answered that it would not offend anyone. I told her that I was grateful to belong to an organization, namely the kingdom of heaven, that authorized its leaders to preside only in that format and that I did not feel like a second-class citizen to be so presided over, even by someone less educated, less experienced, or less wise than myself.

"Yes, but that is the ideal," she said. "Whoever really achieves that? My husband sure isn't at that level."

"Right," I told her. "This life is a training situation. You also will have a chance to practice this style of leadership as a parent and in Church callings. Both of you need all the support from each other you can get to master this skill."

"But what if he tries to boss me around unrighteously?"

"I can tell from the tone of your voice that the scripture will be fulfilled that promises in such a case an 'amen' to the authority of that man. That is, not only does God withdraw his approval and authority from such a leader, but those the person attempts to lead are likely to resist and rebel so that there is a natural 'amen' to his leadership authority also."

Not only is obedience to the principles of order, unity, and agency required of us if we would be righteous leaders, but we simply will not succeed in our efforts to lead our families if we ignore them.

CHAPTER 4

"LIVE JOYFULLY WITH THE WIFE WHOM THOU LOVEST"

We Latter-day Saints proclaim that man's purpose here on earth is to have joy. (See 2 Nephi 2:25.) It seems clear that the Lord intended that joy, like charity, should begin at home. I have always admired the policy in the Law of Moses that a new bridegroom must be excused from military service and from any business obligations that would necessitate his extended absence from home in order that "he shall be free at home one year, and shall cheer up his wife which he hath taken." (Deuteronomy 24:5.)

The truth of the matter is, however, that some couples would not be blessed by such a policy. The more time they spend together, the more miserable they make each other. The problem in such cases is almost always the failure of one or both to follow the basic rules for successful relationships that the Lord has repeated in every dispensation of the gospel. It has always amazed me that committed Latter-day Saints who would not think of sipping iced tea or fudging on their tithing feel justified in ignoring these principles with impunity. The matter is the more perplexing in that the rewards for keeping the commandments they honor may be deferred until the great day of judgment, whereas the rewards for keeping the commandments they ignore are immediate and evident. I should like to focus upon three such commandments.

Love One Another

The Apostle Paul explained the first in this way: "Be kindly affectioned one to another . . . ; in honor preferring one another;

36

... rejoicing in hope; patient in tribulation; ... bless, and curse not." (Romans 12:10, 12, 14.)

Love is so fundamental a gospel principle that it is almost embarrassing to mention it. It is the single identifying quality of those who love the Lord and serve him—they love one another. (John 13:35.) My only contribution is to point out that this rule applies to the members of Christ's church *even if they happen to be married to each other*.

Probably nothing a marriage counselor can do is more effective than getting a fighting couple to declare a truce for a week and start doing good things to and for each other. To paraphrase James, "Show me your love without your works, and I will show you my love by my works," (See James 2:17.)

Among the most effective "good works" are positive comments on our partner's appearance, personality, and accomplishments, and nondemanding touching. Among the least effective are qualified positives ("You look terrific, and you'd look twice as good if you lost twenty pounds"; "I loved your talk! Considering how little time you spent on it, it went very well"; "That was a good cake—I prefer a moister frosting, but the flavor was excellent"; "I really enjoyed that date—I only wish we did it more often.") Equally ineffective are *demanding* touches (the push, the pull, the grab, the nudge, the restraint).

A person who has decided to obey the commandment to "do good" to his or her spouse would be well advised to find out first what would be considered good by the spouse. For example, one wife would be most impressed if her husband planned the evening out, got the babysitter, ordered the tickets, and so on. Another might find this high-handed and would wish to be consulted and to help in the preparation. Still another would value the spontaneous—"Let's chuck it all and go to the movies tonight; what do you say?"

I have known women who would melt if their husbands brought them an unexpected box of candy; I have known others who would be offended that their husbands didn't support their attempt to cut down on sweets; and I have known still others who would feel that such a romantic gesture was a sly attempt to deflect their attention from the *real* issues in their relationship (whatever those might be).

Men are no easier to please. One might enjoy and appreciate his wife's help on a major project while another would consider her meddlesome. Most men would probably appreciate their wives being more active in initiating sexual activity. Yet some would be offended, threatened, or put off by it.

Have you ever noticed that when couples give each other back rubs, they tend to give the rub they would like to receive rather than the one their partners want? Thus a husband may give his wife a firm back rub that she finds painful and even intimidating, while she gives him a feathery massage that he finds ticklish and unsatisfactory.

So, half of the assignment is diagnostic. No points are awarded for good intentions. To do good to a partner, you have to know what your partner needs and wants and how he or she needs and wants it to be packaged (because packaging is often almost as important as substance in these matters). It is not just that your partner wants to go out with you; the way the date is arranged makes all the difference. It is not just that your partner wants to be kissed—it is how and where.

This is a particularly important and challenging issue when it comes to the most complicated of mutual gifts, conversation. Sometimes the partner who is hungriest for "more communication" wants to get right down to serious problem-solving; sometimes he or she wants to share feelings about things of significance to each; sometimes what is hungered after is light "party" conversation such as you used to have in courtship or such as you share with friends. Often the tricky part is not the subject matter but the style of interaction. ("Why do you always make me feel stupid when we talk?" "I wish you could hear yourself, you sound whiney half the time." "You make every opinion a pronouncement of Eternal Truth; can't we just talk?" "Why are you always so sarcastic?" "Where's your sense of humor? I was only kidding.") My suggestion is to listen carefully to such complaints from your spouse. Instead of defending yourself, try to figure out what you could do to come across in a manner more acceptable to him or her. With good will and a little intelligent effort, it doesn't take long to reshape frustrating exchanges into rewarding ones.

No suggestion in this book is likely to be more consequential than this one if it is acted upon. Not only will it bring immediate improvement in the marital relationship, but it will elevate the spirituality of the person who does it. It is not possible to increase conformity to the core principle of our faith without reaping a spiritual harvest. (For those who feel they are not quite ready for this terrestrial degree of altruism, Paul has offered a transitional motivation: "Therefore if thine enemy hunger, feed him; if he thirst, give him drink: for in so doing thou shalt heap coals of fire on his head." [Romans 12:20.])

Control Your Temper

We read in the scriptures: "Put off all these; anger, wrath, malice." (Colossians 3:8.) "A soft answer turneth away wrath: but grievous words stir up anger." (Proverbs 15:1.)

I am repeatedly amazed at how many first-class Latter-day Saints feel that this commandment does not apply to them. "Oh, sure, I have a temper," one might say, "but I blow off a little steam and ten minutes later I've forgotten about it." "Blowing off a little steam" may involve yelling, threatening, swearing, name calling, throwing things around, and, in some cases, physical abuse of a spouse. All of this is rationalized in any number of ways. Unhappily, many have role models in their parents who were also "short tempered." This means that they grew up believing that even good people (such as their parents) lost their temper. To "make a big deal out of it" now would verge on disloyalty to those fine people. It would be like saying, "I guess my folks weren't so great; they never licked their tempers." Even those who did not hold their parents up as models may yet plead that a bad temper runs in the blood: "All Irishmen have tempers, but it doesn't mean anything. If my spouse would just let it be and not get so upset over it, we could be as happy as my folks were."

Others draw upon the pseudo-scientific philosophy that

holds that if you don't get your feelings out, they will build up and cause ulcers or hives. Actually, scientific research has shown again and again that this theory of anger is ill-founded. The explosive expression of anger has a doubly bad effect. First it is hurtful to others and destructive of trust and intimacy. Second, it feeds upon itself within the person expressing it. That is, expressing anger breeds more anger; it does not eliminate it.

But for the reader of this book there is a third reason more significant than either of the other two. The Lord has defined losing one's temper as a serious sin and commanded us not to do it. This is not a moral refinement just a step or two this side of perfection, but a commandment to cleanse ourselves of a major moral transgression. It is not a single admonition from an obscure source, but a key theme of every body of scripture from every dispensation.

Some months ago a young man came to me and said he wished to have his name removed from the records of the Church. It is not common for such a person to attend the court acting on his request, but this young man did. Among other complaints he wished to place in the record was this statement: "My old man used to beat my mom and us kids regular. He broke my jaw once and another time stomped me and cracked three ribs. He was an awful, foul-mouthed, violent man all the time I was growing up. And all that time *you* people gave him a temple recommend every year, year after year. I don't want to belong to a church that thinks such a man is worthy of a temple recommend!"

The young man was wrong in asking to have his own membership revoked, but he was right in claiming that his father should never have had a temple recommend. Indeed, he should have been dealt with in a court himself. Today's priesthood leaders are a good deal more likely to inquire into such matters than in former years. Yet my observation is that even serious offenders rationalize their own behavior. Asked if they ever treated their spouse or children abusively, they answer, "Certainly not!" with a clear conscience when in fact they are in serious violation of one of the core commandments in the gospel of Jesus Christ.

This does not mean that we cannot express our dissatisfaction or strong opinions or pain, but it means we are to do it without attacking anyone either verbally or physically. This principle is easy to document from the scriptures. (Read the Sermon on the Mount and James 1 and 3.)

The Lord's position on this matter is unambiguous: there is *no* permission for losing one's temper in the circle of those who love and attempt to follow the Savior. The only righteous response to our own temper is to root it out as we would root out any other lust or excess in order to be worthy of the kingdom.

There is another kind of anger that can be just as destructive as explosive loss of control: that is smoldering, unforgiving resentment. For some reason there seems to be a general tendency for temper-losers to marry resentment-hoarders, and for each to feel morally superior to the other. "I get it all out of my system and forget it. After ten minutes I'm ready to kiss and make up, but *that one*—she stays mad for days," versus "I would *never* say or do the things that he says and does in a fit of anger, and I can never forget that they were said, either. They hurt too much." This second kind of anger is the kind that poisons love and drives out the Spirit. It is the antithesis of the Savior's counsel to forgive those who despitefully use you. It ignores the counsel to leave judgment and vengeance to the Lord. Even if the offense against one has been major, it remains a corrosive counter-sin to store bitterness in one's heart over it. Not only good marriages but good people are destroyed by it. It is a tool of Satan.

I vividly remember a case in which a father of five children committed adultery and was excommunicated. His wife, in bitterness, divorced him. Eventually, he worked out his repentance, was accepted back into membership, had his blessings restored, remarried, and is today living a full and productive life. She, on the other hand, was so resentful that she withdrew from the Church and from life. Each of her children eventually ran away to live with their father and his new wife. Now, years later, she is a bitter, empty, lonely shell of a person. His sin against her (and against himself) was great, but it was her sin that destroyed her because she would not repent of it.

So anger in either of its forms is a sovereign enemy of intimacy and joy, and every celestial-bound individual must find a way of dealing with it in a way that is consistent with the requirements of the gospel.

Empathize with Each Other

Paul said, "Rejoice with them that do rejoice, and weep with them that weep." (Romans 12:15.) The principle of empathy is at the core of all satisfactory communication. Each of us hungers for a resonant soul that will affirm our joy and share our sorrow. Yet, in the hurly-burly of life, it is easy to miss our cues or find ourselves in a non-responsive mood. For myself, I have tried to make it a rule that nothing I am doing at the moment outranks my wife's claim upon me when she is joyous or despondent. (This would be far more difficult if she were given to excesses in either direction.) She taught me this by modeling it for me.

There are few things more disappointing than to look forward to sharing some triumph, large or small, with a spouse and then be met with some unfeeling response. Solomon was perceptive when he wrote, "Hope deferred maketh the heart sick." (Proverbs 13:12.)

On the other hand, it is at least as disappointing to reveal your emotional pain only to have your mate unfeelingly try to cheer you up. The last thing anyone wants to hear when he is down is a condescending, "Come on, Honey, don't make such a big thing of it." Paul's advice was sound: "Weep with them that weep." Don't try to explain to them why they are foolish to do so.

This chapter opened with the scriptural imperative "Live joyfully with the wife whom thou lovest." (Ecclesiastes 9:9.) If we are to follow that excellent counsel, it will be necessary to keep the laws governing marital joy. This chapter has outlined three of them: the law of love, the law of mastering anger, and the law of empathy. If any lack joy in their marriage, let them consider which of these laws they may not be keeping — and repent.

CHAPTER 5

"HAVING GIFTS DIFFERING"

Sometimes the differences between a man and his wife are so great and so consequential that they destroy the unity of the marriage. Yet none of us are exactly alike, and certain degrees and types of differences may enrich rather than threaten the oneness of a marital relationship. If God had wanted us to marry people exactly like ourselves, I suppose he would not have insisted that there be two sexes and all of the associated gender differences. He would not have insisted that we marry someone from a different family than our own with different role models, different family traditions, different styles of living together, different scripts for being married. There are probably a variety of reasons that we are not encouraged to marry our twins, but one of them surely must be that the Lord sees value in the greater range of gifts and perspectives that two unique partners can bring to the tasks of marriage and parenthood.

Celebrating Differences

Finding a way to make differences complementary rather than competitive and contentious has challenged not only individual marriages but even the Church from the beginning. Paul was compelled to address the issue in his epistles to both the Corinthians and the Romans. To the Romans he wrote: "We, being many, are one body in Christ, and every one members one of another. Having then gifts differing according to the grace that is given to us." (Romans 12:5–6.)

In his letter to the Corinthians he expanded upon the topic: "Now there are diversities of gifts, but the same Spirit. . . . For as the body is one, and hath many members, and all the members of that one body, being many, are one body: so also is Christ. . . . And if they were all one member, where were the body? But now are they many members, yet but one body. And the eye cannot say unto the hand, I have no need of thee: nor again the head to the feet, I have no need of you. . . . And whether one member suffer, all the members suffer with it; or one member be honoured, all the members rejoice with it." (1 Corinthians 12:4, 12, 19–21, 26.)

This principle is as true in marriage as it is in the Church. Yet I find the principle little understood and less appreciated. Rather, most share the view of Professor Higgins in the musical *My Fair Lady:* "Why can't a woman be more like a man?" (and vice versa, of course).

I confess that at some points in my marriage I have fallen into that same simple-minded error. My own disposition is determinedly cheerful. I am an optimist, always looking on the bright side and feeling that few things are improved by worrying about them. In fact, my wife has had cause to complain that my philosophy toward problems is to leave them alone and hope that perhaps they will go away, or, failing that, to muddle through as best I can and believe that everything will turn out rosy in the end.

I married a wonderful woman who is a meticulous planner, a systematic worker, and a varsity-level worrier. I have not always been sympathetic toward her style of dealing with problems. Frequently I have chided her for making too much of something and counseled her to be more like me — full of optimism and prepared to let things fall out as they will. On at least two occasions, however, I have had it brought home to me that I am fortunate to have bonded myself to someone who is quite different from myself in these ways.

The first occasion came early in our marriage. My wife, who worked as a teller in a bank until our children came, used to keep the family budget. She kept it in a great ledger with seventeen columns across — each a different category with its own monthly allocations and balances. I found her approach rigid and unrealistic and told her that she would probably let us starve if we ran out of money in the "food" column even if we had hundreds of unexpended dollars in the "clothes" column. But what bothered me most was how upset she would become when her columns and rows did not balance perfectly. What a waste of human energy! On one occasion I got so carried away with my ridicule of her frustration that she literally threw the ledger at me and told me that if it bothered me for her to worry about the budget then *I* could jolly well worry about it myself.

Well, I knew we were both responsible, frugal people, so I just paid the bills as they came up and spent what was reasonable. I did not even look at their budget ledger. Everything went well for three or four months until we discovered that I had emptied all of her cushions in each column and had gone $1,200 into the red. I gave the budget back to her with an abject apology. We literally could not afford not to worry about money. Something good came of this experience, however (besides my lesson in humility, I mean): she never went back to a seventeen-column double-entry bookkeeping again. It may have been worth the cost just to get a simplified budget system.

The second occasion was even more humiliating for me because the chastisement came from the Lord. We have a daughter who has been subject during her teens to bouts of real depression. Despite my clinical training, which ought to have taught me better, my attitude toward her was often, "Okay, Sweetheart, don't you think it's about time you picked up your bed and walked?" From time to time this daughter would ask me for blessings to help her, and the Lord was always patient and gracious with her, never once rebuking her or expressing condemnation of any kind. You'd think this would have taught me how to respond myself, and to some extent I did try to learn from these experiences. But on one occasion I shall never forget, I placed my hands on her head and heard myself comforting her with these words: "The Lord has blessed you with at least one parent who understands your suffering and can be a comfort and support to you in times of despair." I knew that I was not that parent. After I had recovered from the rebuke, I was filled with appreciation that I had been fortunate enough to marry a good woman "having gifts differing" from mine "according to the grace" given to her.

Negotiating Differences

While some differences, as we have seen, ought to be celebrated as adding strength and breadth to a marital union, others are potentially destructive and need to be negotiated. For example, husbands and wives frequently come to marriage with widely divergent ideas about such basic issues as how money should be handled, how children should be reared, how affection and sexual feelings should be expressed, what constitutes a decent meal, and how leisure time ought to be spent, just to list a few. In fact, I would go so far as to state flatly and dogmatically that no man and woman ever took the marital vows without having to face many such differences. Couples differ enormously in how they handle the disappointment of discovering that values and views that they assumed every reasonable person held were not shared by their spouse. Feeling cheated is a common response. Many conclude that their spouses are stupid or uncouth or selfish or immature or neurotic or stubborn. Many get into running battles over the issues, draining the relationship of much of its vitality and good will. They get enmeshed in power struggles over whose view is right and whose ideas will prevail. As far as I can tell, just being married in the temple is no protection against these unhappy outcomes.

Yet many couples do find constructive ways to deal with such differences. I believe that failing to charitably resolve these troublesome discrepancies is as likely to destroy a temple marriage as any other threat. By small things are great things (good and bad) accomplished. Paul anticipated this problem and counseled the Saints at Rome: "Be of the same mind one toward another. . . . Be not wise in your own conceits [that is, don't commit yourself to imposing your own view of things on your partner]. . . . If it be possible, as much as lieth in you, live peaceably." (Romans 12:16, 18.)

But in view of deeply held differences, how can this be done? Perhaps this question can be discussed most profitably with the help of a case history. Brother and Sister Patten grew up in fine Latter-day Saint families and married in the Salt Lake Temple after a satisfying, storybook courtship. He grew up in an extended family in which hunting and fishing were the chief male recreations. The days out in the back country alone or with a few good friends were the most valued days of the year, the payoff for working hard the rest of the year. She grew up in a family that did everything together. On Saturday morning her father made waffles; then everybody pitched in to do the chores. After the work was done, they would do something fun together, perhaps swimming if the weather was warm, or having a picnic in the country, visiting some nearby historic site, or going to the movies. Her fondest memories were of family vacations to the various national parks.

You can imagine what happened when these two fine Latter-day Saints married. She grew increasingly resentful of his "abandoning" her and the children several times a year to get away into the back country. She felt that if he loved her and the children, he would want to spend all his free time with them, creating the kinds of family memories for their children that she remembered from her growing-up days. He, on the other hand, could not understand her begrudging him his few days of relaxation. He was constantly comparing her to his mother and aunts and sisters-in-law who supported their husbands' need to "get away." He felt cheated in that he was made to feel guilty for doing what every other male member of his family did with a clear conscience.

You may side with the wife or with the husband, depending on your background. The couple tried to get me to tell them which one was being unreasonable. The reality, however, was that they needed to negotiate a mutually acceptable plan for leisure time that built their sense of loyalty and unity rather than eroded it. Because each had so much invested in the outcome, they were hard bargainers, but eventually they were able to negotiate a limited number of away weekends for him and a similar number of weekends for joint activities. The key to the success of this arrangement, of course, was the change in their attitudes as much as the change of schedule. By listening to each other talk about their childhood experiences and their current needs and by reminding themselves of the importance of their commitment to make the marriage work for each of them, they were able to have mutual goodwill in their compromise. That is, not only did he get to go hunting and fishing a certain number of times but he had her cheerful support in doing it. On his part, when his brothers or friends pressured him to join them for additional trips, he was able to be firm in keeping his commitments to his wife without indulging in self-pity for being "henpecked."

Couples will differ in the issues they need to resolve and the compromises they may come up with, but I have observed that those who are able to resolve their differences have several things in common: (1) They have common sense and a realistic perspective; that is, they are aware that differences are normal and do not necessarily reflect upon the character of one's partner, that the marriage is more important than their differences, and that it is reasonable to expect to compromise in any partnership. (2) They are persons of empathy and goodwill; that is, they have the capacity to give their partners the benefit of a doubt as to their motivation, to put themselves in their partners' place and look at the issue from their perspective, and to forego the temptation to wallow in self-pity or to punish their partners (either actively or passively) because their expectations are not fulfilled.

Note that these are terrestrial, not celestial virtues. I know from experience that they are sufficient to achieve a solid relationship despite normal differences. There are also celestial levels of these same virtues, and on occasion nothing less than the celestial level will serve in dealing with particularly difficult cases. Among the toughest cases are those in which only one partner is willing to try to resolve the differences constructively. Then it may require not only common sense but a godlike perspective on the situation. Goodwill may not be enough: Christlike love may be required. Only Latter-day Saints who are refined, committed servants of the Master are likely to succeed at tasks requiring this level of performance. I have come to think of the term "savior on Mount Zion" as applying to such people.

Saviors on Mount Zion

The term "savior on Mount Zion" is ordinarily reserved for those engaged in vicarious work for the dead. Truly, Saints who selflessly devote themselves to genealogical and temple work deserve the title. They perform Christlike service in lovingly opening the gates of exaltation to others who without their work would not have that opportunity.

But I believe that the term might also be applied to another group of the Saints. These have been called to sacrifice for the sake of saving the living, often of their own household.

I first began to think in these terms as a result of counseling two women who had hard life assignments. The first had convinced her boyfriend to join the Church and one year later to marry her in the temple. Unhappily, the conversion didn't "take," and soon thereafter he returned to his worldly ways, which included all of the minor vices and several of the major ones. They had children who seemed to elect their father's life-style rather than their mother's. I watched this good sister struggle with her rebellious family over the years, and I am ashamed to admit that I had sometimes judged her harshly. For example, if she had asked my opinion, I could have told her before she married him that her husband-to-be was more committed to her than to the gospel. Also, I felt that she had been overly permissive with her children. In short, I self-righteously judged that if she had made better choices (as I had, for example) her life would have turned out better (as mine had, for example).

It eventually became necessary to excommunicate her husband, and in agony of spirit she asked me, her stake president, for a blessing to guide her as to what her duty was under the circumstances. In that blessing I learned a few things that even now make me burn with shame for my earlier spiritual arrogance toward that sister. The Lord told her that she was a valiant spirit in the premortal existence who had volunteered for hazardous duty on earth. Not for her was the safety of a secure marriage to an equally valiant partner. Not for her was the relative ease of rearing naturally obedient children. She had (perhaps rashly) volunteered to live her life in the front lines, as it were, of the continuing battle for men's souls. Twice, the Lord continued, she had been given the option of an honorable release from this difficult assignment. (After the blessing she confirmed this.) Twice she had been on the operating table at death's door and was given the free option of coming home or going back to face her challenging responsibilities. Twice she had squared her shoulders and returned to her difficult family. In the blessing she was told that the Lord loved her husband and her children despite their rebellious spirits and that if they were to have any chance at all it would be because of her Christlike patience and long-suffering with them.

When I took my hands off her head I bowed my head in shame, realizing that I stood in the presence of one of the Lord's great ones, truly a savior on Mount Zion.

True to her promise, she is succeeding against all odds in her mission. To everyone's surprise, her rowdy eldest son straightened out his life and went on a mission. He came back on fire with the Spirit and committed to the gospel. Her second son, who had often stated his intention of playing football instead of going on a mission, was helped by his elder brother and has also completed a successful mission and is headed for a temple marriage. Her daughters are slower to turn around, but I begin to see some softening there. Even her husband, the toughest of all, is beginning to mellow at the edges and to talk about putting his life in order (no action yet, but I am prepared to believe in miracles in this family).

The other case involved a man who came from a stable Latter-day Saint family background and a wife who was a convert. Together they were rearing a quartet of healthy young boys. Their problem was the wife's recurrent bouts with anxiety and depression. We got into her background and discovered that she had been raised by an abusive, alcoholic father and a neurotically sick mother who stayed in bed all the time and let her little girl do all of the cooking and cleaning. She confessed that she was still full of rage at her parents for so badly abusing her and full of envy for others who had experienced a normal, loving family relationship. She said that on several occasions when she had seen little girls being hugged and kissed by their loving fathers in Church she had to get up and leave. "The Lord knew what he was doing," she confessed, "when he sent me only boys to raise. Girls would have been too hard."

Then she turned to me and said, "Where is the justice? How can God pretend to be just and send some little girls into homes where they are loved and petted and made to feel like somebody and others into homes where they are beat and molested and abused and neglected? What did I do in the pre-earth life to deserve such a family?"

I felt inspired at that time to tell her that she had volunteered in the preexistence to be a savior on Mount Zion, to come to a family drowning in sickness and sin and to be the means of purifying that lineage. Before her in that line were generations of ugly, destructive, family relationships. Downstream from her purifying influence every generation would be blessed with light and love. The role of a savior, I said, is to suffer innocently for the sins of others that still others may not suffer. There can be no higher calling.

She knew by the Spirit that what I suggested was true. That perspective gave her the strength to get on with her life. The last time I heard from her she had also exercised her prerogative to purify her line backward through temple work and was working hard on bringing her parents to see the light.

I suspect that many of us, more than most would ever guess, have made such premortal choices and accepted such divinely demanding missions. More than once I have felt impressed to tell a righteous, long-suffering person that although his or her mate had provided legitimate grounds for divorce and a later cancellation of sealing, that it would please the Lord if the person would refuse to abandon the assignment to help shepherd that straying soul back to the fold. Occasionally someone says to me, "But don't I have any right to happiness?" The answer, of course, is that for those of us in the service of the Lord, the happiness comes from the service and from the close relationship to our Master that goes with it. If one is looking for a happy, settled, unchallenging life, one probably ought to choose a different master.

I am *not* suggesting that there are never grounds for separation or divorce. I am suggesting that only the Lord can righteously release us from a responsibility we received from him.

CHAPTER 6

"BE YE NOT UNEQUALLY YOKED"

Although it may be our assignment and commitment to remain in a destructive marriage as a representative of the Lord to our errant partner, there are conditions in which we can be honorably released from that assignment. On this subject Paul wrote: "Be ye not unequally yoked together with unbelievers: for what fellowship hath righteousness with unrighteousness? and what communion hath light with darkness?" (2 Corinthians 6:14.)

Clearly Paul was referring to those who had married outside the Church or who had joined the Church despite their spouse's indifference or hostility to the gospel. Yet many are painfully aware that even a temple marriage cannot guarantee against finding oneself in the situation Paul described.

There are many paths that, though they pass through the veil of the temple, lead eventually to being unequally yoked. I do not speak here of those cases where both stray, but of that special set of temple marriages in which one remains true to the gospel and the other wanders off in other directions.

We should begin by stating as emphatically as possible that every case is different and that no book can substitute for revelation from the Lord in response to fervent prayer or to guidance from inspired priesthood leaders. Without that inspiration, one can never know whether one is dealing with a "Zeezrom" who is capable of repentance and eventually of valor once the Lord catches his attention (see Alma 15:5-12) or with a "Korihor" who may protest repeated repentance but will never truly commit to righteousness (see Alma 30:55). Of the Zeezroms, Paul wrote: "The unbelieving husband is sanctified by the wife, and the unbelieving wife is sanctified by the husband: . . . for what knowest thou, oh wife, whether thou shalt save thy husband? or how knowest thou, oh man, whether thou shalt save thy wife?" (1 Corinthians 7:14, 16.)

The Lord works through his servants. He does not protect them from pain, and he does not guarantee them success. He does reward them richly with his Spirit and with the assurance that they will inherit all things if they remain faithful to their commitment.

Even in cases of serious sin against the marriage, such as adultery, which the Lord specified as sufficient grounds for righteous divorce (see Matthew 19:9), I have seen courageous servants of the Lord persevere to eventual victory.

When the Savior visited the Nephites, he gave them instructions on how to treat one who had been excommunicated for unrighteousness: "Ye shall not cast him out from among you, but ye shall minister unto him and shall pray for him unto the Father, in my name; and if it so be that he repenteth and is baptized in my name [i.e., if he returns to the Church, repentant and worthy to have his former blessings restored], then shall ye receive him, and shall minister unto him of my flesh and blood." (3 Nephi 18:30.)

This advice is given to the Church, but it seems to me to apply equally well to the family and the marriage. If there is hope for repentance, we should not be too quick to exercise our right to divorce but should minister to our errant spouse and shepherd him or her back into the kingdom despite our own bruises as have other servants before us, Christ being the Chief Exemplar.

But there is a case where this is not required of us. There are the Korihors of the world who may, from time to time, profess repentance but whose hearts remain hard and who are dominated by another spirit. Of such situations Paul wrote: "What agreement hath the temple of God with idols? for ye are the temple of the living God. . . . Wherefore come out from among them, and be ye separate, saith the Lord, and touch not the unclean thing; and I will receive you. And will be a Father unto you, and ye shall be my sons and my daughters, saith the Lord Almighty." (2 Corinthians 6:16-18.)

In this verse Paul reassures righteous partners that by disassociating themselves and their children from an unclean influence they will lose no status with their Father but will go on to become his sons and his daughters with every blessing that is implied in that holy designation.

Similarly, Christ told the Nephites to persist in laboring with the repentant sinner, not casting him out. Then he said: "But if he repent not he shall *not* be numbered among my people, *that he may not destroy my people*, for behold I know my sheep, and they are numbered." (3 Nephi 18:31; emphasis added.)

On more than one occasion Christ has compared his relationship to the Church to that of a bridegroom to a wife. It seems to me a legitimate analogy to draw in this case, also. That is, if a spouse's transgressions continue and he or she shows no genuine repentance, if the physical, emotional, and spiritual well-being of the family is endangered, "he shall *not* be numbered among my people, *that he may not destroy my people*." In plain English, there is a time to leave such a spouse with the blessing of the Lord. But I should reiterate that such a departure is like the "reproving betimes with sharpness" alluded to in section 121 of the Doctrine and Covenants: it needs to be qualified always by the phrase, "when moved upon by the Holy Ghost." (D&C 121:43.)

Moreover, having made the break, thus protecting ourselves from the destructive influence of this transgressor, it does not necessarily follow that we have no further responsibility toward him or her. Although this is a high and demanding standard, the Lord continues in his admonition to the Nephites: "Nevertheless [even after you have withdrawn membership from him], ye shall not cast him out of your synagogues, or your places of worship, for unto such shall ye continue to minister; for ye know not but what they will return and repent, and come unto me with full purpose of heart, and I shall heal them; and ye shall be the means of bringing salvation unto them." (3 Nephi 18:32.)

I realize that the family's situation is not quite the same as the congregation's; in this case the analogy breaks down to some degree. There is nothing in the family that is quite the equivalent of the nondemanding, low-risk admission to public services at the synagogue. But the intent of the scripture is clear, and the principle applies in both cases. It is not good to designate our former spouse as the enemy who is to be ostracized and vilified. A true servant of Christ will continue to wish the spouse well and to do anything within the bounds of good judgment to make it easier for him or her to return to the Lord, if he or she later elects to do so. Rarely is the formerly victimized wife (or husband) and family available for reunion and living happily ever after at that point. Life moves on. New circumstances and commitments arise. Often there is no putting Humpty-Dumpty back together again, but there is no need for bitterness or vindictiveness either. Both corrode the souls of those who indulge in them. It is entirely possible to set clear and reasonable limits on the type and frequency of contact between the family and the destructive, unrepentant spouse and yet not partake of these counter-sins.

The Lord has promised again and again that if we do our part, nothing that anyone else can do has the power to deprive us of the blessings of the kingdom. Those who, through no fault of their own, are deprived of a worthy eternal companion will be provided for. I am aware that this promise does not comfort many. As one good woman said to me, "I don't want to be assigned to some man, however worthy, that I don't even know." My faith is that God not only will provide for us, but that he will provide for us in ways that bring us unalloyed joy. There will be no reluctant Saints trying to put a good face on a second-class choice. Whatever our final assignment, it will be not only just and merciful, but it will be beyond imagination, for "eye hath not seen, nor ear heard, neither have entered into the heart of man, the things which God hath prepared for them that love him." (1 Corinthians 2:9.)

To illustrate this general set of principles in more detail, let me briefly cite three cases.

The Andersons were a high-powered LDS couple. Both

had held executive positions in their ward and stake, and both held responsible, well-paying jobs. Sister Anderson came to me troubled because over the past three or four years her husband had become "flakey,"

"What do you mean flakey?" I asked.

"Well," she replied, "he's in a business where even the most ethical men fish in murky waters sometimes, but increasingly he is getting just plain dishonest. He misrepresents what he is doing with the money people give him to invest, and I can't tell you how many people—old friends and even relatives—have complained to me that he has lied to them or taken advantage of them. He was always a sharp business man, but he has gone beyond sharp to dishonest."

"Have you talked to him about your feelings?"

"Yes, but he just slams out of the house and says I don't understand business, which is baloney. I may not know the details of his business, but I've been in the business world for seven years and I know that what he's doing is just plain wrong. If he gets caught, we'll lose everything, but that's not the point. The point is that he holds a temple recommend and he shouldn't. I can't stand being married to a man who isn't going to be able to take me to the celestial kingdom. He may fool the bishop, but he's not going to be able to fool the Lord."

As often happens, this problem was compounded with others. Her husband had also become increasingly enamoured with Eastern mysticism and owned a growing library of books on the subject. He had come to believe that "the Mormon Church has only a small part of the whole truth. These people have an understanding of the powers that are in man and in the universe that far transcends anything they have even guessed at in the Church Office Building in Salt Lake City." His wife, at one point, felt such an unholy spirit about these books that she threw them all away while he was on a business trip. When he returned he was so enraged that he hit her and moved out of the house for a month. Eventually, he agreed to return only if she promised to let him replace his library and respect his beliefs. She relented and he moved back in, but shortly thereafter she came to see me. "I hate the spirit he brings into our home," she said. "I was more at peace with myself and with my Heavenly Father while he was gone. What should I do? It's a temple marriage and I don't want to do anything wrong, but I just can't continue to be this man's wife."

Eventually this couple did divorce. The husband's financial tangle is in the courts, and, pending the resolution of that litigation, a Church court may be in the offing. Her decision to leave him (much delayed because of the financial complications of trying to negotiate a divorce settlement in the midst of all of the other problems) was based on her finally coming to the prayerfully anchored conclusion that he was unrepentant and unreachable over a long period of time, and that he was literally under the influence of an evil spirit and that she did not want herself or her teenage children to continue to be exposed to this influence. Her bishop and stake president have supported her decision. Others, including the husband's parents, have criticized her, accusing her of deserting him when he needed her most. But I am persuaded that she has made the correct decision after going through the appropriate steps. She appears to have been married to a Korihor, and there was little to be gained and much to be lost by prolonging the association.

In another case, a husband came to see me. He had recently been disciplined by a Church court for becoming physically involved with a secretary (he did not commit adultery, but his behavior was inappropriate, and he knew perfectly well that he had no business doing what he did). He felt particularly bad about this because he held a responsible Church position and felt he had disappointed some people who meant a lot to him. He told me that he had no excuses but that in explanation he had a very difficult marriage. His wife was a demanding woman who had virtually cut off any affection to him and who was both verbally and physically abusive to him and to their children. I met with them both individually and jointly for a number of months. She had had a bad childhood and had a long series of complaints about her life from that period through their marriage. In the course of our sessions she never tried to improve herself but constantly complained about her husband, people at Church, and the way therapy was going. (She had strong opinions about most things, including how I should conduct our sessions, what I should tell her husband, and how the stake president should have handled the court.) On various occasions she threatened suicide, locked her husband out of the house, and even attacked him with a skillet and with scissors. The provocation in each case was refusing to do what *she* felt he should do. The final blow came when she bruised one of her young children so badly (for not minding) that she was reported by the school counselor as a child abuser. This led to the final breakup and divorce. The husband was awarded custody of the children and has been reinstated into full membership in the Church.

As a therapist, I recognize that this woman had severe emotional problems and that she needed help. But, having worked with her for nearly a year, I will say that it cannot be assumed that everyone who needs help accepts help. In her pain she elected to rehearse her grievances over and over without taking any responsibility for her own behavior. At no point was there any glimmer that she was allowing the Spirit of the Lord to work with her (despite her "strong testimony of the gospel" and regular temple attendance throughout much of this period). She was unforgiving, petulant, and abusive. I do not say that she had no cause for resentment. But I do say that she treasured it rather than trying to find ways to let it go. This is as destructive of a relationship with the Spirit as many more frequently mentioned sins, and I, for one, felt that her husband's decision to leave her was fully justified within the context of the scriptures we reviewed in the first section of this chapter.

In the third case, the wife was an intense, bright, committed, hard worker, and he was a pleasant, easy-mannered Nice Guy. He had done well in his career and had always been active in the Church, but he never had the follow-through for a key position. He was always some dynamic person's not very dynamic counselor. For a few years he served on the high council of his stake. His stake president kept shifting his assignment every few months, trying to find the niche where he would take hold and produce. Finally he was retired to the ward. Meanwhile, his wife was the fire behind half of the things that happened in the stake on the women's side. They had what I have called a "magpie/mole" marriage. That is, she, magpie-like, was always cawing and pecking at him to try to get him to do more and be more, and he, mole-like, was always burrowing more and more securely into a hole of passivity. Then in their mid-forties he confessed to her that he was having an affair with a woman at work.

She was furious and devastated. By the time of the Church court, though, she had reevaluated the whole thing and decided that part of the fault was hers and that she was going to fight for their marriage. She attended the court as a witness on her husband's behalf. Their stake president referred them to me as part of their post-court regimen. The husband was repentant, and they worked hard on building their relationship. Eventually he was permitted back into the waters of baptism and a few months later his blessings were restored. On their last visit to me, she said, "I never thought I would ever say these words—no one could have convinced me of it two years ago—but I am glad this happened. As a result of it, we talk more than we ever did, we are closer than we ever were, and there is more of the Spirit of the Lord in our home than there has ever been."

He put it less elegantly: "Some folks are like the mule in the story—you have to get their attention with a two-by-four before you can teach them anything. I guess my mistake and the court finally got our attention."

This woman had every right and reason to leave her husband. But she chose to work with him instead. The result was not the reachievement of the old status quo—it was the creation of an altogether new level of union and satisfaction. That is not always the result of the choice to stick it out after one partner's transgression. Often it is very difficult to get the damaged heart of the relationship pumping again. But if both parties commit to the effort in righteousness, forgiving and learning from the experience, success is the lawful and natural result. In such a case the couple do not end up unequally yoked because they have learned to pull together in their harness.

CHAPTER 7

"ART THOU LOOSED FROM A WIFE?"

Paul obviously was troubled by how to advise those with broken marriages in his day. We cannot fully appreciate his advice for the Saints in that time and place because we are not fully aware of their circumstances. Much of what he counseled in the seventh chapter of 1 Corinthians (verses 8-40) seems not to apply to our present-day circumstances nor to correspond with the guidance of contemporary Church leaders. But some of his opinions (which he went out of his way to label as *only* his own opinions—not the word of the Lord) may serve as a provocative starting place for our discussion: "Art thou bound unto a wife? seek not to be loosed. Art thou loosed from a wife? seek not a wife. But and if thou marry, thou hast not sinned. . . . Nevertheless such shall have trouble in the flesh." (1 Corinthians 7:27-28.)

Then, as now, apparently, marriages among true believers sometimes floundered. As we noted in the previous chapter, there are more acceptable and less acceptable reasons for becoming "loosed" from a mate. Temple marriages are several times more stable than marriages for this life only, but they too may end in divorce and leave the survivors beached on the shores of the connubial seas.

It is important not to forget that divorcés are not a homogeneous group. Their circumstances vary enormously. Some have finally resolved a prolonged emotional trauma that dragged on for years. Some naively find themselves caught by surprise and can scarcely believe the reality of their unwelcome situation. Some have been the (mostly) innocent partners of an erring spouse. Some have suffered Church court action as a result of their own transgression. Some are young, some are older. Some have enough to live on, some are destitute. Some have young children to care for, some are totally alone. Some determine to follow Paul's counsel and remain single, and of those, some do and some do not. Others are anxious or even desperate to find a mate who will love, comfort, and be true to them, and among those some find what they are looking for and go their way rejoicing; some find a new relationship that turns out (as Paul forewarned) to be "trouble in the flesh" — a frustrating repetition of the disappointment of their first marriage; and some find no one at all.

Having counseled with hundreds of divorced Latter-day Saints as a priesthood leader, a therapist, or a participant in a Special Interest fireside or retreat, I can report that while they differ in many ways they also share certain opinions. The first is that this is not an easy church to belong to if you are divorced. Church activities, both sacred and recreational, are usually structured for whole families. The lessons and sermons and literature presuppose not only a whole but a happy family. And the damning banner invisibly strung across every Church entryway says this: *"No other success can compensate for failure in the home."*

The second observation is that it is a tough world out there, morally, for divorcés. Most report that they found it a good deal easier to resist sexual temptation in the innocence of their virginal youth. Now that they have become accustomed to an active sex life, it is more difficult. They tell me that they find virtually no support for the ethic of postmarital chastity in the world (where it may actually be viewed as a neurosis) and that even Church-sponsored Special Interest activities provide no real sanctuary. There, as elsewhere, one may sometimes encounter the predatory (or perhaps only lonely and desperate) man or woman who makes no bones about being sexually available.

In marshaling one's resources to cope with these temptations, it does not help that they come at a time of unprecedented loneliness and vulnerability. Often one's feelings include a tinge of bitterness also. Many divorcés believe that not only their former spouse but also their friends, family, Church leaders, and even God have treated them badly. As a result, some have become disillusioned and resentful. I remember one woman who told me: "I did it all like I was supposed to. I believed what they told me as a Laurel, and I dutifully fought off the whole priests quorum at one time or another. I waited for my missionary. I married in the temple. I tried to be a good wife. And for what? Where are the rewards I was promised all my life? Now I'm getting the same old song from my bishop and my sister: 'Be good and God will bless you.' Well, I'm sorry, but I just don't believe that anymore."

Thus, for a variety of reasons, many who were the relatively blameless partner in the original divorce, later become unworthy of a temple recommend. Whether the transgression came during or after the marriage, I urge each son and daughter of God who find themselves in this situation to turn away from their self-destructive course and return to the path that leads home. If such a person has developed an unholy life style, he or she must change it. If such a person has quit paying tithing, he or she must pay it. If such a person has a lover, it is necessary to give him or her up. If a Church court is needed, it should be sought out. The Lord set up his judicial system as part of the process of repentance for a sound purpose. We must trust him. We must submit to him.

In return, it is not promised that our trials will be removed. It is promised that our prayers will begin to clear the ceiling once more, that we will begin to have the gifts of the Spirit manifest themselves in our lives again, and that we will rediscover the feeling of inner peace and eternal safety. As those in this circumstance will already have discovered for themselves, these are not small gifts.

Remarriage

The Apostle Paul noted, "If thou marry, thou hast not sinned." (1 Corinthians 7:28.)

I assume that no one, as they knelt at the altar in the sealing room, ever imagined that at some future time they might be doing so again with a different partner. The marriage was to have been for eternity. Yet there they are again.

As Paul indicated, if the Lord considered them sinnners, they would not be at that altar. Whatever sins may have been committed have been dealt with, and they are in the temple because two judges in Israel have interviewed them in depth and pronounced them worthy.

Remarriages, as Paul also hinted, are subject to special strains beyond those of first marriages. My counsel is to avoid comparison (even positive comparisons) with the former spouse or situation at any cost. The closest I would ever let myself get to that would be a statement such as, "Boy am I glad that you finally came into my life!" which implies an appreciative comparison but avoids calling forth the Ghost of Anniversaries Past.

As for triangles, the temple remarriage, like any other, may have to deal with the often conflicting interests and claims of current spouse and former spouse, children from the various unions, and such persons as former mothers-in-law, former spouse's new mate, current spouse's former mate, and a whole cast of auxiliary characters. But temple remarriages also have issues unique to themselves. I refer, of course, to the question of sealings.

When a couple who have been sealed in the temple get a civil divorce, all marital rights, duties, and claims upon each other are terminated so far as this life is concerned. For example, if they were to have sexual relations with each other after the divorce is final, it would be considered fornication and grounds for a Church court. Yet the civil divorce is powerless to touch their eternal bond. Only the same power that forged that bond can loose it. As Christ said to Peter, "Whatsoever thou shalt bind on earth shall be bound in heaven: and whatsoever thou shalt loose on earth shall be loosed in heaven." (Matthew 16:19.) Those keys have always been held by the First Presidency.

I once talked with a woman who was divorcing her husband on grounds of general incompatability. I asked her how she felt about still being sealed to him for eternity. She replied, "Oh, that suits me fine. I'm not anxious to marry anyone else, and I figure that if he makes it to the celestial kingdom he'll have been perfected and so will I, and we'll have no problem being together. If one or the other of us doesn't make it, there is no need to worry about it at all."

I am not sure what the Lord's view of that is, but her reasoning has a certain logic to it.

On the other hand, most divorcing couples have generated enough bad feelings toward each other that the thought of being eternally sealed to each other is repulsive. One man put it succinctly when he said, "I can't tolerate being with her here. My idea of the celestial kingdom sure isn't being stuck with her forever."

Some couples are of such a practical disposition that this sort of thing bothers them very little. Others are disturbed by unfinished celestial business hanging over their heads. As one woman put it, "Well, I just hope that they do get this straight in the millennium because there is no way I am going to share him with *that woman!*" To which her husband added, "Amen!"

A still more difficult problem arises with the sealings of the children. To whom will they belong in the eternities? To their father and his new wife? To their mother and her new husband? To the original father and mother despite their subsequent divorce? To the grandparents on the mother's side who were faithful Latter-day Saints (given that no one in the parental generation qualifies and the grandparents on his side are not even Church members)? The *Temple President's Handbook* and the *General Handbook of Instructions* outline the policies governing the wide variety of circumstances that parents and children may find themselves in with respect to sealings. I will not attempt to review these complex guidelines here, but I do have two suggestions for a remarrying couple. First and foremost, any Latter-day Saint who is worthy of a temple recommend should be spiritually mature enough to refrain from using the sealing issue as a wedge between family members. I am thinking of the sort of argument that includes such zingers as, "If you really loved me, you would want to have my children sealed to you!" or "When you act like that, I'm glad I'm not sealed to you!" It is a serious sin to use a sacred ordinance as a blunt instrument to hurt someone with.

Second, trust the powers of heaven not to make stupid or insensitive "celestial arrangements" for us. None of us need fear that what is important to us may not be important to God and that we may be arbitrarily forced into situations that would be repugnant to us.

CHAPTER 8

"TO GIVE UNTO THEM
BEAUTY FOR ASHES"

When Jesus determined that it was time to declare his Messiahship and inaugurate his ministry, he traveled back to preach in his "home ward" in Nazareth and chose Isaiah 61 as his text. That scripture reads, in part: "The Spirit of the Lord God is upon me; because the Lord hath anointed me to preach good tidings unto the meek; he hath sent me to bind up the brokenhearted, ... to comfort all that mourn; ... to give unto them beauty for ashes, the oil of joy for mourning, the garment of praise for the spirit of heaviness." (Isaiah 61:1-3.)

Few people on the day of their temple marriage would suspect it, but some will have the opportunity to participate in that healing ministry within their own marriages. Usually, we view our newly acquired eternal companion through the traditional rose-colored glasses, and our whole idea of the gospel and its effects on people's lives is likely to make this idea foreign to us. We are likely to feel confident that if we keep the commandments (and we intend to) then we should experience sustained joy. And joy is the opposite of the "spirit of heaviness" referred to in Isaiah.

For these and other reasons, it is especially difficult for us Latter-day Saints to deal with depression when it comes—either to us or to our spouses. In speaking of depression I am not speaking of disappointment or "down" days when we feel a little out of sorts and in need of cheering up. I am referring to clinical depression, one of the most devastating of all emotional illnesses. Despite the feeling among many that it should have no place in a home where the Spirit dwells, this problem is as commonly found among us as among any other people.

In earlier days depression was known as melancholia. Other terms associated with it are despondency, despair, hopelessness, worthlessness, bitterness, and cynicism. It is truly a disease of the spirit as well as of the mind. Those afflicted, therefore, feel not only pain but guilt. How could such a thing come upon them unless in response to terrible sin? And after the guilt, shame: How could anyone be attracted to our faith with our example before them? Where is that joy that is supposed to be the hallmark of the righteous marriage?

Probably the two best documented cases of biblical characters who suffered from extended clinical depression are King Saul and King Solomon (apparently nobody bothered to document the emotional problems of lesser folk). There was a temporary bright spot in King Saul's case when it was discovered that his profound melancholia responded to David's musical therapy. But the story turns out badly. Despite David's soothing music and his loyalty, forgiveness, and patience, Saul's illness escalated from melancholy to paranoia and finally to violence and self-destruction.

Solomon's case was less dramatic but more eloquently documented, since we have a whole book of scripture, the twelve chapters of Ecclesiastes, as a record of his depressive thinking. Anyone who has experienced real depression should read these chapters, not so much for solace or solutions (for some, at least, Solomon's solutions seem too pat to be convincing) but just to see the painfully familiar themes of world-weariness, despair, futility, and cynicism expressed with such literary flair. I have included a few examples. They cannot do justice to this magnificent dirge, but they may, perhaps, convey the flavor of it. Here is Solomon, "the Preacher," at his most depressed.

On wisdom:

> I the Preacher was king over Israel in Jerusalem.
> I have seen all the works that are done under the sun;
> and, behold, all is vanity and vexation of spirit. That which is

crooked cannot be made straight: and that which is wanting cannot be numbered.

And I gave my heart to know wisdom, and to know madness and folly: I perceived that this also is vexation of spirit. For in much wisdom is much grief: and he that increaseth knowledge increaseth sorrow. (Ecclesiastes 1:12, 14-15, 17-18.)

On laughter:

I said in mine heart, Go to now, I will prove thee with mirth, therefore enjoy pleasure: and, behold, this also is vanity. I said of laughter, It is mad: and of mirth, What doeth it? (Ecclesiastes 2:1-2.)

On achievement:

I made me great works; I builded me houses; I planted me vineyards: I made me gardens and orchards, and I planted trees in them of all kind of fruits: I made me pools of water, to water therewith the wood that bringeth forth trees: I got me servants and maidens, and had servants born in my house; also I had great possessions of great and small cattle above all that were in Jerusalem before me: I gathered me also silver and gold, and the peculiar treasure of kings and of the provinces: I gat me men singers and women singers, and the delights of the sons of men, as musical instruments, and that of all sorts.

Then I looked on all the works that my hands had wrought, and on the labour that I had laboured to do: and, behold, all was vanity and vexation of spirit, and there was no profit under the sun. . . . Yea, I hated all my labour which I had taken under the sun: because I should leave it unto the man that shall be after me. And who knoweth whether he shall be a wise man or a fool? yet shall he have rule over all my labour wherein I have laboured, and wherein I have shewed myself wise under the sun. This is also vanity.

Therefore I went about to cause my heart to despair of all the labour which I took under the sun. (Ecclesiastes 2:4-8, 11, 18-20.)

On the nobility of man:

And moreover I saw under the sun the place of judgment, that wickedness was there; and the place of righteousness, that iniquity was there.

70

I said in mine heart concerning the estate of the sons of men, that God might manifest them, and that they might see that they themselves are beasts. For that which befalleth the sons of men befalleth beasts; even one thing befalleth them: as the one dieth, so dieth the other; yea, they have all one breath; so that a man hath no preeminence above a beast: for all is vanity. (Ecclesiastes 3:16, 18-19.)

On hard work:

As he came forth of his mother's womb, naked shall he return to go as he came, and shall take nothing of his labour, which he may carry away in his hand. And this also is a sore evil, that in all points as he came, so shall he go: and what profit hath he that hath laboured for the wind? (Ecclesiastes 5:15-16.)

On scholarship:

And further, by these, my son, be admonished: of making many books there is no end; and much study is a weariness of the flesh. (Ecclesiastes 12:12.)

On the hope of eternal life:

For to him that is joined to all the living there is hope: for a living dog is better than a dead lion. For the living know that they shall die: but the dead know not any thing, neither have they any more a reward; for the memory of them is forgotten.

Whatsoever thy hand findeth to do, do it with thy might; for there is no work, nor device, nor knowledge, nor wisdom, in the grave, whither thou goest. (Ecclesiastes 9:4-5, 10.)

By contrast, in the New Testament, although depressive thoughts are acknowledged, the emphasis seems to be on hope. For example, Paul, without question, had his down times, but he seems to have handled them far more constructively than Solomon. On one occasion he became quite upset with the members of the branch at Corinth, which he had founded. It had come to his attention that they were comparing him unfavorably to other teachers and were particularly critical of him for having cancelled a promised visit to them. He reacted with indignation, reminding them of all of the things he had suffered for them and for the gospel's sake. The list is impressive. (See chapters 11 and 12 of 2 Corinthians for a dramatic cataloging of all he had been through.) But despite all that he suffered at the hands of both friend and foe, his hope remained bright. He wrote: "We are troubled on every side, yet not distressed; we are perplexed, but not in despair; persecuted, but not forsaken; cast down, but not destroyed." (2 Corinthians 4:8-9.)

Paul's formula for avoiding despair had three parts:

1. Taking a long-term perspective:

> For our light affliction, which is but for a moment, worketh for us a far more exceeding and eternal weight of glory; while we look not at the things which are seen, but at the things which are not seen: for the things which are seen are temporal; but the things which are not seen are eternal. (2 Corinthians 4:17-18.)

2. Focusing on what can be done to change rather on how terrible things are:

> Now I rejoice, not that ye were made sorry, but that ye sorrowed to repentance: . . . for godly sorrow worketh repentance to salvation . . . : but the sorrow of the world worketh death. (2 Corinthians 7:9-10.)

3. Placing one's hope in Christ:

> And he [Christ] said unto me, My grace is sufficient for thee: for my strength is made perfect in weakness. (2 Corinthians 12:9.)

As he put it in his letter to the Romans, "Who shall separate us from the love of Christ? shall tribulation, or distress . . . ? Nay, in all these things we are more than conquerors through him that loved us. For I am persuaded that neither death, nor life, . . . nor height, nor depth, . . . shall be able to separate us from the love of God, which is in Christ Jesus our Lord." (Romans 8:35, 37-39.)

On another occasion Paul apparently learned that his good friend and protegé Timothy was discouraged and floundering in his new calling as bishop of Ephesus. Paul's counsel was direct and inspiring: "I put thee in remembrance that thou stir up the gift of God, which is in thee by the putting on of my hands. For God hath not given us the spirit of fear; but of power, and of love, and of a sound mind." (2 Timothy 1:6-7.)

It is not recorded how Timothy responded to this encouragement. If his problem was mere discouragement it probably had a positive effect upon him. But if he was the victim of clinical depression, it is my seasoned opinion that it only made him feel worse.

Paul's inspired (and inspiring) three-point program and his attendant counsel is powerful medicine for many who suffer from discouragement, but the unpalatable truth is that no clinically depressed person I have dealt with has ever been able to take nourishment from that sort of scripture. Rather, they feel condemned by it.

I remember once being invited to help give a stake president a blessing between the sessions of general conference because he was in such depths of depression that anything the Brethren said appeared to him to be damning. In the blessing the Lord spoke words of comfort, love, hope, and forgiveness to this good man. The Spirit in that room was palpable, the veil was thin. I and the other brother assisting had a powerful witness that this man's overwhelming sense of unworthiness was totally unfounded and irrational. Yet some months later, after he had worked his way back to good mental health, this brother confessed that at the time all he could think was, "How can these good men dare to lie like that in the name of the Savior? I suppose they are only trying to be helpful."

This is not an uncommon response. Truly depressed people cannot stand to go to Church or read the scriptures because they feel that every word is a fiery dart. As one told me, "At the lowest point you believe in hell but not in heaven." Shades of Solomon!

Perhaps the reader will conclude that such a frame of mind could only be the result of sin. None of us are without sin, and it certainly does appear that depression feeds upon and magnifies our imperfections, but I would stack my depressed

Latter-day Saint clients against any comers on the final judgment day.

There is ample evidence that several of the prophets in the Book of Mormon suffered from bouts of melancholia. Nephi wrote: "Notwithstanding the great goodness of the Lord, in showing me his great and marvelous works, my heart exclaimeth: O wretched man that I am! Yea, my heart sorroweth because of my flesh; my soul grieveth because of mine in- iquities. I am encompassed about, because of the temptations and the sins which do so easily beset me. And when I desire to rejoice, my heart groaneth." (2 Nephi 4:17-19.)

Jacob wrote: "The time passed away with us, and also our lives passed away like as it were unto us a dream, we being a lonesome and a solemn people, wanderers, cast out from Jerusalem, born in tribulation, in a wilderness, and hated of our brethren; . . . wherefore, we did mourn out our days." (Jacob 7:26.)

In our own dispensation Joseph Smith, as ebullient a spirit as ever wore the prophetic mantle, yet had his dark times (see, for example, D&C 121:1-6), and Spencer W. Kimball has documented from his own journal his recurring battle with melancholia. On the occasion of his call to the apostleship, he went into a four-month slough of despondency during which he wept every day, doubting the propriety of his call. He referred to this period as his own Gethsemane. (Edward L. Kimball and Andrew E. Kimball, Jr., *Spencer W. Kimball* [Salt Lake City: Bookcraft], 1980: pp. 188-95.)

Outside of the Church, perhaps no one has earned more respect as a man of God and of good than has Abraham Lincoln. Yet he was tormented with profound depression throughout much of his adult life.

The point of all this is threefold. First, depression is not the wages of sin. Good men and women, and even great ones, may be afflicted with this condition. Second, depression is peculiarly resistant to the sorts of uplifting advice and reassur- ance that are often helpful in cases of mere discouragement. Finally, depression is not a short-term problem; it requires patience of a caliber that can survive not days or weeks but often months of emotionally draining disability.

Surviving and Overcoming Depression in a Temple Marriage

Next to seeing an eternal partner fall into transgression, probably nothing is more upsetting than watching them drown in an apparently bottomless pool of depression. People who feel that bad frequently think and talk about suicide. Their faith turns sour, and they can't seem to pull themselves together to achieve *anything*. When "anything" includes going to work or taking care of the children, depression can put enormous strain on the relationship. Probably the most common, the most natural, and the most destructive error in dealing with depression is to think of it as being voluntary. Usually those who are depressed are encouraged to count their many blessings, to compare their favorable circumstances to those of others who have *real* problems but don't sit around all day feeling sorry for themselves, to repent of their self-pity and pull themselves together, to pick up their bed and walk! They are reminded that God loves them, that their patriarchal blessing promises great things for them, that if they will only place their burden on the Lord, he will bear it for them. At length, after a spouse has patiently explained all of this several dozen times without effect, he or she is likely to get discouraged or even disgusted with the nonresponsive mate.

It does not help that depression not only cuts down on a person's ability to pull his share of the marital workload, but it also virtually eliminates the sex drive.

But depression is not voluntary. I cannot believe that *anyone* would choose to suffer the black pain of despair or elect to stay in the hell of utter hopelessness one hour if they saw themselves as having any choice at all. In fact, to some degree depression affects the will. It makes it difficult for the sufferer even to decide to get out of bed to go to the bathroom. Asking someone to overcome the depression itself is like asking him to move a skyscraper.

The depressed know that they cannot overcome their depression themselves and yet they tend to reject any help offered.

This brings me to the second basic error often made by Latter-day Saints whose wives or husbands suffer from depression. When the affliction does not seem to yield readily to prayer or to the laying on of hands or to faith-promoting testimony, people have a tendency to withdraw from these activities and from the afflicted spouses. They are not ones to cast their pearls. But although their depressed mates may not receive such ministration gracefully and although they may seem not to be responsive to them, *yet they need this sort of spiritual care more in the midst of their depression than at any other time*. Later they may well describe those apparently futile gestures as the things that kept them alive, that sustained them through their bitterest moments of despair.

The third issue is the sheer length of time that a depressive episode can last. Untreated, a full-blown clinical depression is likely to last anywhere from three or four months to two years! There cannot be many spouses whose patience is calibrated to that kind of time frame.

Depression does respond to treatment, however, and I cannot recommend too strongly that professional help should be sought early rather than late. There are generally three components of successful treatment: medication, talk-therapy, and spousal support.

Medication. Next to the Christian Scientists, there is probably no group in America more leery of medication than Latter-day Saints. I am not altogether sure why this is so, but in the case of depression, it is a misplaced value. Whatever else may be involved, depression is a biochemical event in the body. The brain actually runs slower because of certain deficiencies in the system. There is a pharmacopoeia of thoroughly tested medications to remedy this imbalance. In my opinion, it is criminally negligent to withhold such medication from a depressed person on the grounds of some personal disinclination—as much so as if the disease were diabetes or leukemia. I know that many in the Church would prefer to treat all such matters through "natural" nutritional means. Good nutrition is of benefit to anyone. I recommend it. But it is *not* a substitute for professionally supervised medication.

Talk-therapy. There are always ideas in the depressed person's mind that become the anchors of his despair. A skillful therapist who shares or respects the client's values can be very helpful in sorting through such ideas.

Spousal support. Spouses hold the key to overcoming and avoiding depressive episodes. First, their patient love and reassurance is the most valuable single resource next to the gospel of Jesus Christ that the depressed person has. At appropriate times a faithful spouse can help his partner reestablish contact with the Spirit through prayer, provide priesthood blessings, and bear testimony. In an earlier chapter I cited Paul's advice to "rejoice with them that do rejoice, and weep with them that weep." (Romans 12:15.) That is excellent counsel for a spouse helping a troubled mate in the early stages of depression. That is, initially nothing is more valuable for the despairing spouse than to feel empathy and understanding. The depressed do not need or want jollying. Later, affectionate teasing might be effective. At the darkest stages, no form of humor, however gentle, will be appreciated by the person. But there comes a point when humor may be an important tool in helping him or her make it all the way back to well-being.

Supporting the person in following doctor's orders, taking medication regularly, and keeping therapy appointments will pay off in a faster and more sustained recovery.

In my experience, most depressed people will respond within a few weeks to the treatment suggested in this chapter, thus cutting months off of the anticipated duration of their problem.

In achieving a solution, the couple is likely to learn a new appreciation for the insufficiently valued virtue of patience and learn new depths of meaning for the counsel that he who would be saved must endure to the end. And although it may not touch the heart of the depressed partner when in the depths of despair, both partners will come to a unique appreciation of the Savior's willingness to experience himself all of the pain that we might experience and to show us the path through it to eternal life. Paul wrote: "Wherefore in all things it behoved him to be made like unto his brethren, that he might be a merciful and faithful high priest in things pertaining to God, to make reconciliation for the sins of the people. For in that he himself hath suffered being tempted, he is able to succour them that are tempted. . . . For we have not an high priest which cannot be touched with the feeling of our infirmities; but was in all points tempted like as we are, yet without sin." (Hebrews 2:17-18; 4:15.)

To Joseph Smith, in the midst of his deepest despair, the Lord said: "The Son of Man hath descended below [all tribulations]. Art thou greater than he?" (D&C 122:8.)

And on another occasion, in referring to his own pain in Gethsemane and on the cross, he said: " . . . which suffering caused myself, even God, the greatest of all, to tremble because of pain, and to bleed at every pore, and to suffer both body and spirit—and would that I might not drink the bitter cup, and shrink—nevertheless, glory be to the Father, and I partook and finished my preparations unto the children of men." (D&C 19:18-19.)

Such is the God that we worship. Such is our Helper when the unfathomable blackness of despair is upon us and we feel otherwise alone. Such is the Partner at our side as we succor a loved one through the valley of the shadow.

CHAPTER 9

"BEHOLD A LADDER SET UP ON THE EARTH, AND THE TOP OF IT REACHED TO HEAVEN"

We know from our own experience that to set our feet on Jacob's ladder is not to have reached the top of it. Although our goal is heaven, our preoccupations are too often of the earth, earthy. Yet the inverse is also true. Though we may be mired in the most mundane carnalities, yet it makes a great difference that our hearts are set on heaven. With that commitment it becomes possible to convert even troubled temple marriages into celestial unions. It seems to me that in addition to the particular principles that pertain to particular problems, there are two or three general principles that are central to our success.

The first principle is that ladders must be climbed one rung at a time. If we are to achieve perfection at all, it must be step by step, "line upon line." One clear implication of this is that no matter how far we may find ourselves from our goal, our duty is to reach for the next rung up and begin to climb.

The second principle is that if we will make that initial effort, the Lord will intervene with additional knowledge and help. As he told Nephi, "I will give unto the children of men line upon line, precept upon precept, here a little and there a little; and blessed are those who hearken unto my precepts, and lend an ear unto my counsel, for they shall learn wisdom; for unto him that receiveth I will give more; and from them that shall say, We have enough, from them shall be taken away even that which they have." (2 Nephi 28:30.)

I have been impressed by how the Lord kept that promise with a series of young men who came to me with homosexual problems. At first, the possibility of ever being back on the track to the kingdom with a temple marriage and normal lifestyle seemed so far away to them that they could only contemplate it with despair. But step by step, they reached that goal. First, they learned how to deal with their negative feelings toward themselves. Gradually, they came to realize that they were of worth, whatever their life-style or afflictions. Next, they learned to conform to the commandments, even if only in a mechanical way. By the time they were living worthy to go to the temple, the Lord began to work a mighty change in their hearts. In each case, separately, they began to dream romantically about women and to discover the stirrings of attraction toward the opposite sex while losing feelings of attraction toward their own. Next, for each, the Lord raised up a good, patient woman who loved well and was easy to love in return. As each has said, "This has been a series of miracles!" The key is in the word *series.* Each miracle built upon the one before it. By contrast, those who prayed, however fervently, for the miracle from the beginning, never received it, and if they were not willing to try the experiment of faith, step by step, they became bitter against God for his refusal to answer them and turned again to their former life-style. It is so with us all. We may well be awed by the size of the task before us, which, after all, is nothing less than achieving perfection as a couple. But if we begin by correcting the obvious flaws that are well within our power to correct, the Lord will give us the extra strength or wisdom—and if necessary a miracle—to proceed toward our righteous goal. I have seen that occur in the lives of literally hundreds of couples.

This brings us to the third principle, which is that different qualities of motivation are required for different levels of the ladder. Many of the problems we have discussed are basically telestial problems—selfishness, insensitivity, greed, pride, lust. Yet even those mired in such weaknesses are not beyond the touch of the Spirit that would lead them upward. In my experience, the Lord takes people at whatever level he can get their attention and leads them from lower to higher ground.

I am reminded of Alma's careful nourishing of the dim

light of faith he found among the outcast Zoramites, to whom he said: "If ye will awake and arouse your faculties, even to an experiment upon my words, and exercise a particle of faith, yea, even if ye can no more than desire to believe, let this desire work in you, even until ye believe in a manner that ye can give place for a portion of my words." (Alma 32:27.)

Even among the most worldly of my clients I find motivation to change their lives for the better. The Savior pointed out that even publicans love those who love them (Matthew 5:46), and that sinners will cheerfully give to other sinners in the expectation of receiving as much in return (Luke 6:34).

A couple who has taken temple vows ought surely to begin at a higher level of moral maturity, but I, for one, will take them at whatever rung of the ladder they may find themselves on, given only a commitment to improve.

If ever I am tempted to doubt the wisdom of this philosophy, I recall a couple (again, as it happens, a bishop and his wife) who had developed a vicious cycle in which he criticized almost everything she did (or failed to do); when this happened, she would withdraw into a rebellious pout that might last for days. They had come by their strategies honestly, having grown up in families where they had seen no other form of marital interaction. (The fact that outside of their home each was looked up to as a model Latter-day Saint did not help the marriage. They resented the fact that their spouse was wonderful everywhere but where it mattered.)

They were unusually difficult to entice away from their habitual, mutually destructive pattern. He could see that if she would just listen to his well-intended suggestions, he would have less to complain about. She could see that if he would support her instead of being hypercritical, she would feel like doing more and being more of a wife to him. Each thought the other party was unfair and immature. They felt bad about their own behavior but felt that it was simply a reaction to the other partner's faults.

After several weeks of listening to fruitless counter-complaints, I finally persuaded the couple to at least consider alternative responses to their partner's bad behavior. At first I

ONE FLESH, ONE HEART

would take her role and dare him to try to force me out of my more assertive but noncombative response. Then I would take his role and see if she could provoke me into his usual patterns of criticism. Then they practiced new responses in my office and finally were assigned to "try the experiment of its goodness" at home for seven days. It did not go perfectly, but it worked well enough to force them to admit that some such effort *might* improve their home life. Once the initial barrier was broken, the positive elements in their relationship increased until the marriage became the most rewarding part of their lives rather than the most demeaning and painful. But beyond that, the change in the atmosphere made it possible for the Spirit of the Lord to dwell in their home for the first time in their lives together. After a few weeks of this, the wife said a peculiar thing; she said, "I feel married—really married for the first time." She meant, I think, that she was beginning to feel of one flesh and of one heart with her husband.

In this couple's case, they moved from a telestial relationship through terrestrial on the way toward celestial in a very few months. Usually the change is more gradual. When a husband and wife in a bitter power struggle come to see me, I presume that my first task is to move them to the terrestrial level, that is, to a level based on goodwill, self-discipline, and honor in keeping commitments. This style of interaction, as virtuous as it sounds, is not celestial since it requires no faith in God, no eternal covenants or ordinances, no hope in the Atonement, no Christ-like love. In short, it is the level of honorable men and women, which the Lord has labeled terrestrial.

Yet I rejoice when this level is achieved. It is a great thing to overcome willfulness, stubbornness, temper, pride, and lust. To have achieved honor in keeping commitments and goodwill toward each other is enough, I am sure, to make the angels sing. As the Savior said: "Joy shall be in heaven over one sinner that repenteth, more than over ninety and nine just persons, which need no repentance."(Luke 15:7.)

But for those of us who have covenanted to follow the Light, to seek life instead of death, that can never be enough. It is not enough to move from mutual neglect and criticism to mutual supportiveness. It is true that such a couple might complement each other, help each other, touch each other tenderly, and tend to each other's needs. This would be heaven, you say? True. It is the heaven represented by the glory of the moon. The celestial law requires not merely mutual support but a commitment to help each other back to our Father's presence: "Husbands, love your wives, even as Christ also loved the church, and *gave* himself for it." (Ephesians 5:25; emphasis added.)

It is not enough to put away petty malice and violence and temper tantrums and to become even-handed and just in all our dealings with each other. This is required, but it is only the foundation of a celestial esteem for each other. As Paul put it, "Let all bitterness, and wrath, and anger, and clamour, and evil speaking, be put away from you, with all malice: and be ye kind one to another, tenderhearted, forgiving one another, even as God for Christ's sake hath forgiven you." (Ephesians 4:31-32.)

It will not serve merely to overcome divisiveness and con-tention and insincerity and to be willing compromisers and honorable truce keepers. The goal is to become one. And there is only one way to achieve that unity. Each must become one with Christ while becoming one with each other. That is what Christ petitioned the Father for on the eve of his crucifixion. After praying for unity among the apostles he was about to leave behind, he continued: "Neither pray I for these alone, but for them also which shall believe on me through their word, . . . that they may be one, even as we are one."(John 17:20, 22.)

To achieve this, we must be born again and become celes-tial people. The path to the kingdom leads through our own living rooms and bedrooms. Step by step, rung by rung, may we, with God's grace, refine our lives and our marriages until we have achieved that celestial union that is our intended destiny and our home.

INDEX